Three Songs, Three Singers, Three Nations

The William E. Massey Sr. Lectures in the
History of American Civilization 2013

Three Songs, Three Singers, Three Nations

GREIL MARCUS

Harvard University Press

Cambridge, Massachusetts

London, England

2015

First printing

Library of Congress Cataloging-in-Publication Data

Marcus, Greil.

   Three songs, three singers, three nations : the William E.
Massey Sr. lectures in the history of American civilization
2013 / Greil Marcus.

      pages cm

   Includes bibliographical references and index.

   ISBN 978–0–674–18708–5 (cloth : alk. paper) 1. Folk
songs, English—United States—History and criticism.
2. Dylan, Bob, 1941– Ballad of Hollis Brown. 1964.
3. Lunsford, Bascom Lamar, 1882–1973. I wish I was a mole
in the ground. 1928.   4. Wiley, Geeshie. Last kind words
blues. 1930. 5. Folk musicians—United States. I. Title.

   ML3551.9.M37 2015

   782.421620092—dc23   2015010873

For Bill
a writer's reader

CONTENTS

ILLUSTRATIONS

Three Songs, Three Singers, Three Nations

Inflection
"Ballad of Hollis Brown," Bob Dylan

It's May 1963, and John Henry Faulk is back on the air. It's been six years. He was born in Austin, Texas, in 1913; entranced by African-American sermons, he came out of the University of Texas with a degree in folklore—with a name like John Henry, he almost had to become a folklorist, or a character in his own folk song.

Against his will, he did become that character. As the host of *Johnny's Front Porch* on CBS radio in the early 1950s, he was the latest version of Will Rogers, telling southern stories and passing on homilies. In New York he appeared on TV game shows, and crossed paths with Alan Lomax and others in the leftist milieu of professional folk music. The blacklist was everywhere, in every field, promulgated by the White House, Congress, the FBI, in entertainment by movie studios, television and radio networks, and especially by watchdog groups like Counterattack, with its constantly updated guide *Red Channels.* In 1955, Faulk, the CBS newsman Charles Collingwood, and dozens more formed an anti-blacklist slate and ran for seats on the board of the American Federation of Television and Radio Artists; in a bitterly fought campaign, they swept the election.

The next year Faulk was himself blacklisted as a Communist by a group calling itself Aware. His sponsor dropped him. CBS cancelled his show. But Faulk, unlike the blacklisted folk singer Pete Seeger, had never joined the Communist Party or followed its line. With Louis Nizer as his attorney, Faulk sued Aware for libel; when after six years the case finally came to trial, Faulk won. He more than won: the jury's award of $3.5 million—more than $25 million today—was a break in the wall the blacklist had built around the entertainment industry. Faulk published his memoir *Fear on Trial* in 1964, and went on to a featured role on the CBS country-music vaudeville show *Hee Haw;* he lectured at colleges on the Constitution. On television, he played, among other characters, Strom Thurmond; in the movies he played the Storyteller in the original *Texas Chainsaw Massacre,* and Pat Neff, the Texas governor who in 1925 pardoned Lead Belly, after the great folk singer and convicted murderer sang

Neff a song pleading for release, and not without a sting: "If I had you, Govnor Neff / Like you got me / I'd wake up in the morning / And I'd set you free." Faulk died in 1990; in 1995 the Austin Central Library was renamed in his honor. But in 1963, Faulk played a role that, at least in the moment, might have given him the most pleasure of all. He was hosting a show for the Westinghouse Broadcasting Company: *Folk Songs and More Folk Songs!*

It's the height of the folk revival. The collegiate faces of the Kingston Trio have erased the old, automatic identification of folk music with the Communist Party and the Popular Front. "Communism," went the official 1930s party slogan, "is twentieth-century Americanism." Party cadres, among them the classical composer Charles Seeger, the father of Pete Seeger, and later of the folk singers Mike Seeger and Peggy Seeger, under his *Daily Worker* name Carl Sands—as if he were fronting for Carl Sandburg himself—made folk music the fanfare of the common man. It was a story that continued without any real interruption through 1950, when the Weavers, led by Pete Seeger, had a number-one hit with a cleaned-up version of Lead Belly's "Goodnight, Irene"— before they too were blacklisted and their career was destroyed.

Some people threw their Weavers albums away; some hid them. But now, in 1963, there are folk music clubs all over the country, and folk music albums all over the charts: by the end of the year Peter, Paul & Mary's *In the Wind,* closing with their version of Bob Dylan's "Blowin' in the Wind," will be number one, and Dylan's original, as carried on *The Freewheelin' Bob Dylan,* will crack the Top 40. For tribes of young people all over the country, the Newport Folk Festival is the center of the universe. Joan Baez has been on the cover of *Time. Hootenanny* has just made its debut on CBS, notably without John Henry Faulk, its natural host. It will be a huge hit—instantly reviled for its ban on Pete Seeger, which would lead to a boycott by Baez and many others, it will be cancelled before the end of 1964.

Faulk's show—taped a month before *Hootenanny* first aired—could have been meant as a counter in advance. It opens with a cartoon of a train running through a landscape of desert and mountains. The whistle toots. "This train goes flyin' by," sings a cheery, accentless chorus for the WBC version of Woody Guthrie's "This Train Is Bound for Glory"—his train didn't carry "no big shot ramblers," but there's no need to bring up the anti-capitalist catcalls here. We see the windows of the train filled with the happy faces of people holding guitars and throwing their heads back in song. "Folk music!" says an unseen announcer with a typically confident, colorless TV voice. "It's in the air, everywhere!" We see folk singers perched on the tops of skyscrapers. "The voice of freedom—the *cry* of despair. The *shout*"—we see a farmer with a banjo surrounded by a cow, a pig, and a duck—"of the land." A guitar-and-banjo-picking family of six drives through a tunnel cut into a giant redwood. "The sound," we hear, "of a growing country. The good"—a singing sailor on a skiff—"the cheerful"—a wailing two-guitar couple singing on a couch while their dog looks up from the floor—"the sad"—there's a close-up in the cartoon of the dog looking sad. "The sound—of America."

We see the singers we've been hearing: the Brothers Four, who had a number-two hit in 1960 with "Greenfields"—it will be on the radio for years—smiling, clean-cut strummers posed against the desert backdrop and earnestly singing Lead Belly's "Rock Island Line." We hear the train pulling to a stop; steam from the brakes washes over the screen. "The Brothers Four!" says the announcer, as they grin even more widely than before. "Bob Dylan!" A year earlier, he'd lined out an unrecorded song about Faulk, "Gates of Hate," a surviving fragment of which—"Go down, go down you gates of hate / You gates that keep men in chains / Go down and die the lowest death / And never rise again"—sounds like fifteen-year-old Nathan Zuckerman's skin-crawlingly self-righteous radio play "The Stooge of Torquemada" in Philip Roth's *I Married a Communist;* now he strolls across the set, tipping an invisible hat. "Barbara Dane!" and the deep-voiced singer follows. "The Staple Singers!" and twenty-three-year-old Mavis Staples leads her two sisters, her brother, and her father across the stage.★ "And

---

★ Dylan and Mavis Staples had met at a gospel music festival in New York the year before. It was in a way a dream come true. "It just went through me like my body was invisible," Dylan said in 2015 of hearing the Staple Singers' "Uncloudy Day" in 1956, tuning in late at night from Hibbing, Minnesota, to a station in Shreveport, Louisiana, stunned by Pop Staples's otherworldly tremolo guitar playing. "I looked at the cover and studied it," he said of finding a Staple Singers LP with the song on it. "I knew who Mavis was without having to be told. I knew it was she who was singing the lead part," he said. "Mavis looked to be about the same age as me in her picture . . . And I said to myself, 'You know, one day you'll be standing there with your arm around that girl'"—and he said, looking over his shoulder from 2015 to 1963, "there I was, with my arm around her." Backstage at the

Carolyn Hester!" the announcer says finally—in
1961 Dylan had backed the Texas folksinger on
harmonica for a Columbia session that led to his

Faulk show, with everyone present, Dylan asked Pop Staples for her hand in marriage. "Don't tell me," he said,
"tell Mavis." Not long after they began an affair that
lasted for years. "My lost love," Staples said in 2013, "because I didn't go and marry him. I was just too
young"—and, as Greg Kot quotes her in *I'll Take You
There: Mavis Staples, The Staple Singers, and the March Up
Freedom's Highway,* "It was always in my mind that I
couldn't marry a white guy." They had a reunion in 2003;
to close the tribute album *Gotta Serve Somebody: The
Gospel Songs of Bob Dylan,* the two combined for a rou-
tine based on "Jimmie Rodgers Visits the Carter Family"
and "The Carter Family and Jimmie Rodgers in Texas,"
skits recorded in 1931. Dylan is singing his "Gonna
Change My Way of Thinking" with a band, his voice one
great sore throat, when he breaks off: "Why, look, someone's coming up the road, boys." There's a knock on the
door. "Hey," someone says, "it's Mavis Staples." "Oh,
good to see all of you," says Staples in a voice that if anything is scratchier than Dylan's. "My goodness, Bobby,
got a nice place here." "Thank you, Mavis," Dylan says,
and they go into a long, fierce, joyous version of the gospel
standard "I'm Gonna Sit at the Welcome Table" with
hammering funk backing. "Well, we living by the Golden
Rule," they declaim. "Whoever got the gold rules." In
2013, Jeff Tweedy, who had produced Mavis Staples's albums *You Are Not Alone* (2010) and *One True Vine* (2013),
was with his band Wilco touring with Dylan; he told him
Mavis had asked him to say hello for her. "Tell Mavis she
should have married me," Dylan said.

own contract with the most prestigious record company in the country. "And your narrator, John Henry Faulk!"—and as the Brothers Four pack up their instruments, a man in a suit with a pipe in his mouth ambles into view.

He's carrying what looks like a salesman's sample case, which he sets down on a table, right there out in the desert of the set. "Well, glad to be back again this way, folks"—it's not a casual thing to say, not with six years of oblivion behind him, but his heavy drawl smothers any trouble. Immediately he's a circuit-riding country judge, down-home, plain-folks in a patently phony way that no one we've glimpsed before has been. Yes, he's glad to be back again this way, folks, and, he goes on, "back with one of America's finest products"—and you think he's going to open the case and demonstrate a Westinghouse broiler, or maybe a fan. "Freedom!" he says: *that's* the product. Faulk pounds the case three times with his pipe hand. "Of course," he says, "freedom isn't really in the *bag*." What's going on here? Is he saying that freedom is in jeopardy? That it's not a done deal? Because of the kind of people who came after him? Yes, he won the case, but he's not back on CBS yet, the *Hootenanny* Pete Seeger ban is in the news—isn't

Faulk pushing his luck? "Not exactly," Faulk says, his hand over his heart. "It's in our hearts, and our *minds*"—and in 1963, on television, for a show about a subject as happily populist but lingeringly suspect as folk music, even the word *mind* can translate as critical thinking, dissent, disloyalty, pointy-headed intellectualism, communism. "But I thought," Faulk says, his drawl broader than ever, "maybe today, we'd show you a few pictures here"—he gestures at his case—"have our friends sing you a few songs. Maybe your hearts and minds can do the rest, get us caught up in that great American dream." He opens the case. There's a cartoon of a Yankee-doodle-dandy fife and drum trio.

After a commercial, we see Faulk leaning back, his pipe now a tool of contemplation. "I been poking around this land of ours for quite a spell now, takin' some long looks at it—well, some short ones, too. And I'll say this: that as a *nation,* we might have our shortcomin's, we've done some *mighty fine things. Mighty fine* ones. And I reckon that's because we got off to a *great start,* with the—declaration about *freedom,* and *rights of man.* That's the thing that's guided us through all these years." He gazes into the distance; off camera, there's a sprightly harmonica. We might not have recognized Bob Dylan's sound in 1963, but we do if we're looking at the old tapes now. "Hear that?" Faulk says as his ear catches the instrument, his face nearly tearful with satisfaction: *"Ahhhhhh!"* He looks even more deeply into the big sky of the western set. He's at once unbearably and irresistibly corny. "Whatever we've done as a people," he says, his voice now that of the country sage, the old man who's been all around this land, "it's always been turnin' up in *song. Folk songs,* we call 'em," Faulk says, both including and excluding the viewer, gazing higher still into the studio sky—*these songs are about you, but you're not part of this* we *yet, you don't really know what I'm talking about, but maybe what I'm going to show you will give you a clue*—and as the harmonica turns plaintive, distant, Faulk pushes the point: "I don't guess there's a better way in the world to get to know about a country, and its people, than to listen to its songs." He nods his head thoughtfully; there's a fade to Bob Dylan, singing "Blowin' in the Wind." He sings it modestly; he turns and walks off against a background of clouds.

It's the setup to an extraordinarily ambitious show: it means to trace the whole sweep of American history, and it does. As the cartoon unrolls, the Civil War is fought, and the West is won; wagon trains cross the continent. There are farmers and cowboys; the Brothers Four do "Rodeo." There are shoot-outs straight from the opening of *Gunsmoke*. We see factories and railroads from coast to coast—and two cowboys, one holding a torch, looking up at the feet of a black man, dangling in the air. "The Negro was tantalized with just a *taste* of freedom. He still sang his songs about the joys of heaven, rather than the songs about the joys of"—Faulk nods his head—"this earth." The Staple Singers appear, the women in prayer gowns, Mavis leading the group through "Little David" with a deep, burred voice, Pop Staples ringing his electric guitar, tipping them into "I Just Got to Heaven." Cartoons show class war, bosses and unions. Against a mountain backdrop, Carolyn Hester sings "Payday at Coal Creek," followed by Dylan, an oil derrick behind him, with "Man of Constant Sorrow," an old folk song he'd recorded for his first album, *Bob Dylan,* released the year before. The story charges on: immigrants remake the country. The First World War ("Shoulda been the last," Faulk says) breaks into the Roaring Twenties, with cars, jazz, blues—with Barbara Dane singing "Nobody Knows You When You're

Down and Out" and Bessie Smith's "Backwater Blues"—and then the crash.

Now we see whole populations of homeless people, and a truck emblazoned "California or Bust." The Brothers Four start up Woody Guthrie's "Pastures of Plenty"—and despite how little they can bring to it, it works. It's too good not to. And then straight into Bob Dylan, off camera, singing "Hollis Brown, he lived, on the outside of town / Hollis Brown, he lived, on the outside of town," as the camera pans oddly to the left over a cartoon tableau of forbidding, snow-topped mountains jutting up from alkaline sands. The camera eye is brought down to the studio desert floor, where you see the white, weathered skull of a cow, an image taken from an iconic Marion Post Wolcott Farm Security Administration photo, shot in Lame Deer, Montana, in 1941.

Still trained on the ground, the camera moves to the right, until it rests on the shadowed boots and jeans-covered lower legs of an otherwise unseen figure, holding for a full ten seconds before it even begins to pan up to Dylan's face, which it takes more than twenty more seconds to reach—and when you see his face, it betrays no sign that anything this melodramatic has

been going on. He is concentrating on putting the song across. He doesn't look at the camera. He is not signaling with his eyes or his mouth. There is no expressive body language. He is not emphasizing anything. "Your baby's eyes are crazy, they're a-tuggin' at your sleeve / Your baby's eyes are crazy, they're a-tuggin' at your sleeve" is presented flatly. The melody, formed on Dylan's strummed guitar, backed by an offscreen banjo—familiar but out of place, out of reach—is insistent, pushing forward as a kind of moral monotone. The monotone says that when one speaks of things such as these, this is how one must speak, without affect, so that the truth can speak for itself. The insistence is a denial that life was ever any different, or ever will be.

The song moves on, and as the cartoon landscape disappears into a black backdrop, you are brought into the story: a failing farm, a starving family, a father who ends the story, his and that of everyone else. It sounds as much like Dylan's own song as "Blowin' in the Wind," and, without its arty self-consciousness, as much like a commonplace, handed-down folk song as "Man of Constant Sorrow." The small, everyday details dig into your mind as they pass, the contours of the song are primal, epic, and the singer stands behind the song, to the side of it—whether he is seen facing the camera or shown in profile, the song is always in the foreground, the singer less its performer than its medium. "You prayed to the Lord above, oh please send you a friend / You prayed to the Lord above, oh please send you a friend," but no one hears, no one listens. The grass is dead, the well is dry, the flour is black from rats, the horse is mad—the picture is as elemental as the one drawn in Béla Tarr's *The Turin Horse,* where the line between existence and death is so thin neither the characters in the film nor the people watching them in a theater can recognize it. The only specifics in the song are "Hollis Brown" and "his wife and five children," in the first verse, sung as you're still looking at the singer's feet, and "South Dakota farm," said twice in the last verse—and those three words stick, coming off the rest of the song, a fact in the face of a fable, throwing you off.

You had the comfort of letting the singer lead you through an allegory, an archetype, and now he's not. Now, with those three words, he's saying something else: this happened, and, against your own will, you are convinced that it did. Maybe you knew, maybe you forgot, maybe you read about it, maybe you didn't, but which would be worse, that you forgot, or that you never knew? Somehow the burden of sin has shifted from the man who killed his family and himself to you, the listener, because as the song moves forward, you are the friend the man prayed for, the person who pretended not to listen, who pretended not to hear. Dylan raises his guitar, finishes the song, and walks off. Faulk walks the show through FDR, Hitler, the Atom Bomb, and a cartoon of women and children turning fearful faces to the sky. "Makes all war seem a little silly, now," he says. Carolyn Hester sings "Last Night I Had the Strangest Dream"— that the world "agreed to put an end to war."

"*Welllll*"—not quite *waaaal,* but not quite "Well," either—"we held on to our freedom," Faulk says at the close of the show, the whole night's company gathered behind him on a stage floor painted with a map of the country. "And along with it, we got some other things, too. Automatic brains, that think for us. Frozen pizza pies, rockets to the moon, television, detergents, *food stamps!* And a couple of problems"—the drawl deepens, as if to say, *Who says there's a problem we can't solve?*—"the Russians," Faulk says, "and the Red Chinese. We've accepted a lot of responsibility in this new world of ours, for a lot of people—but I think we're going to be able to live with it, just like we always have." A loud strum comes up from the Brothers Four guitarist, and everyone is singing a bright, denatured "This Land Is Your Land," in 1940 Woody Guthrie's response to Irving Berlin's "God Bless America." By 1963, along with "We Shall Overcome," it was the national anthem of the folk revival; nine years after that, George McGovern would recite it as he accepted the nomination of the Democratic Party for president of the United States. "You see," we hear Faulk off camera, more laconic than ever—he sounds as if he's leaning against a barn—"freedom is still our business, same as it ever was. We've protected it from the gunslingers, a couple of other power-hungry folks, and we're still guarding it, still facing challenges. Well, we've always done pretty good, in the past"—by now the charm has faded, and if you're still listening you don't believe a word you hear—"what of the future? Well, that's up to you. Whatever we do, we'll sing about it." A Dixieland trumpet rises over the sound as the Brothers Four keep on with "This Land Is Your Land," and Faulk strolls to the front of the set with his pipe raised to his chest as he mouths singing along. In deep background, you can make out everyone else gathered in a line at the back of the stage, all singing, Bob Dylan standing alone, in the center, strumming the song—but not as he played it at the Carnegie Chapter Hall late in 1961, as a dirge, a performance that gives the lie to every sound now coming out of Faulk's mouth: a horribly slow, defeated, all-our-dreams-are-in-the-past performance that gives the lie to the song itself.

It was an early, unanswerable, shocking version of the way, in Bob Dylan's rewriting and re-singing of American song—from his first recordings, three teenagers feeding quarters into a machine in a St. Paul music store on Christmas

Eve in 1956, singing doo-wop songs off the radio, to the last show Dylan played, as I write, on December 3, 2014, at the Beacon Theater in New York, closing with "Blowin' in the Wind" and "Stay With Me," a Jerome Moss–Carolyn Leigh composition Frank Sinatra recorded in 1965 that Dylan somehow turned into a version of Stephen Foster's "Hard Times"*—of

---

* I was lucky to be there, on a night where there were many centers of gravity, where songs took on a new depth, where you could hear them as unfinished stories— of a piece with what Dylan did on November 23, when, before a show in Philadelphia, he played a four-song set for a single audience member (a Swedish TV stunt), and the highlight was a slow, ruminative version of Fats Dom- ino's "Blueberry Hill" so full of death it would have sounded just right on his *Time Out of Mind*. At the Beacon, the first crack in the ice that can form around familiar songs came with "Workingman's Blues," the melody pulled out, the pace ground down—all a look back, to when the word *workingman* had some dignity. Here the "sing a little bit of these workingman's blues" hit home, because now that's all anyone can expect: nothing. "Pay in Blood" came off like a Clint Eastwood spaghetti western. "Tangled up in Blue" was a novel, seeming longer than any time before, truly tangled, turning into the rambling yarn of "New Danville Girl." Dylan stretched lines out. "*Soooooon* to be divorced"' took plea- sure in pure music-making—and it was the first hint of the expansive, four-lane-highway voice he was holding in reserve. "Lovesick" had a harsh, south-of-the-border

the way a simple inflection, a change in the pressure brought to bear on certain words, stretching a phrase, flattening a melody, stepping away from an obvious or seemingly necessary rhythm, refusing to let an image that has already appeared in outline come completely into focus, can change everything. A change in

---

feel, a sense of the nighttime opening of *Touch of Evil.* "Highwater" was almost a comedy by comparison— because it really is funny. But it was the comedy of a flood survivor sneering at those who didn't make it: this song will never hit bottom. There was the violin-led chamber music of the great "Forgetful Heart"—its roots in Arthur Smith's 1938 "Adieu False Heart" came to the surface as never before. There was "Scarlet Town," a mystery about time and place where "the streets have names that you can't pronounce"—and the guy who's telling you this was born there. The killer was "Long and Wasted Years." It was presented as such, with Dylan strutting back and forth, setting the stage for something big. And it was big—the music, but mostly the voice. It was bigger verse by verse, huge, then enormous, then too big for the hall, not a crack in tone, a voice that wore the lives it had lived like old clothes, a voice with a hint of snake oil—the carny barker of the gods, the medicine show pitchman whose stuff really does cure all ills, but can also strike you dead, because it can tell the wheat from the chaff. It was fun, it was transporting, with the feel of a Davy Crockett or Abe Lincoln tall-tale teller in there too—I rassle wildcats, I drink the Mississippi dry, I bring the house down.

inflection—in the singing, on the guitar, with causes that can only be identified by their effects—can reverse meanings, breathe life into clichés, kill off characters that for anyone else would be happily rolling down an open road.

What makes Dylan's 1961 performance of "This Land Is Your Land"—sung at a time when he was visiting Woody Guthrie as he wasted away from Huntington's chorea, singing Guthrie's own songs to him—is put across in his understated but cruelly hard cadence, in the way that each line of the song is sung as a single, complete sentence, each phrase on the guitar big and solid, so that as Guthrie describes how, as he walked the highway, he saw it mirrored in the "endless skyway," the phrases are broken up into pieces of an idea, fragments of a voice calling out to each other, each piece—"California," "the New York Island," the redwoods, the Gulf of Mexico—now in its own exile, long since scattered, ideas that will never connect again. *This land was made for you and me*—as Dylan played it that night, it reaches the heart as *This land is not your land. This land is not my land. And it never was.* I heard a recording of that 1961 performance in 2012, as exit music for a new staging of *Of Mice and Men,* coming on just after, for the last time, George tells Lennie about the farm they'll have together—"Look acrost the river, Lennie, an' I'll tell you so you can almost see it"—right before George shoots Lennie in the back of the head.

This is "Ballad of Hollis Brown," as it was sung on Bob Dylan's third album, *The Times They Are A-Changin',* released in January 1964.

> Hollis Brown
> He lived
> On the outside of town
> Hollis Brown
> He lived
> On the outside of town
> With his wife and five children and his cabin
>   broken down
>
> You look for work and money
> And you walked a ragged mile
> You look for work and money
> And you walked a ragged mile
> Your children are so hungry that they don't
>   know how to smile
>
> Your baby's eyes look crazy
> They're a-tuggin' at your sleeve

Your baby's eyes look crazy
They're a-tuggin' at your sleeve
You walk the floor and wonder why with every
    breath you breathe

The rats have got your flour
Bad blood it got your mare
The rats have got your flour
Bad blood it got your mare
Is there anyone that knows, is there anyone
    that cares

You prayed to the Lord above
Oh please send you a friend
You prayed to the Lord above
Oh please send you a friend
Your empty pockets tell you that you ain't
    a-got no friend

Your baby's a—cryin' louder now
It's pounding on your brain
Your baby's a—cryin' louder now
It's pounding on your brain
Your wife's screams are stabbin' you like the
    dirty drivin' rain

Your grass it is turning black
There's no water in your well

Inflection

Your grass it is turning black
There's no water in your well
You spent your last lone dollar on seven
    shotgun shells

Way out in the wilderness
A cold coyote calls
Way out in the wilderness
A cold coyote calls
Your eyes fix on the shotgun that's hangin' on
    the wall

Your brain is a-bleedin'
And your legs can't seem to stand
Your brain is a-bleedin'
And your legs can't seem to stand
Your eyes fix on the shotgun that you're holdin'
    in your hand

There's seven breezes blowin'
All around the cabin door
There's seven breezes blowin'
All around the cabin door
Seven shots ring out like the ocean's pounding
    roar

There's seven people dead
On a South Dakota farm

There's seven people dead
On a South Dakota farm
Somewhere in the distance there's seven more
    people born

In this book I am looking at three commonplace, seemingly authorless songs as bedrock, founding documents of American identity. These songs can be heard as a form of speech that, with a deep foundation, is always in flux. This may be especially true in the work of Bob Dylan, over what is now nearly sixty years, where a single performer can be seen to have taken the whole of this tradition and translated it into a language of his own. It's a language that, by now—as it has been taken up by other artists, such as Todd Haynes, with his 2007 film *I'm Not There,* a movie filled with Dylan-like figures, composites and specters, played by at least four men, two women, and a fourteen-year-old African-American boy—has itself become a form of the commonplace: a language anyone can speak, as if it were common coin, no one holding more rights to it than anyone else.

There is a language in the American folk song that, as people speak the same phrases as everyone else, seduces or compels them to add their own shadings, their own cues, elisions, emphases, stresses, images, twists, highlights, effacings, so that any statement can appear at once as commonplace and individual, something anyone might say in a way that no one else would ever say it—a language that allows people to find their own voices, and then disappear into the crowd. A language in which there is, at the source, no original—and if there is no original, there is no copy. Each statement is a thing in itself, and not a thing at all. It's someone at a city farmer's market doing his or her own, faithful, Alan Lomax–songbook versions of "John Henry" or "Wreck of Old 97," with its engineer "scalded to death by the steam"; it's Jon Langford of the Mekons on an NPR stage in 2003 singing his "Lost in America," where, to the most stirring tune imaginable, Langford's voice melting with empathy and regret, "John Henry laid his hammer down / And headed back to his hometown / But someone turned the signpost round / Someone took the road sign down / He didn't want to make a scene / He died in the wreck of the C 19 / Scalded to death by the dream." The C 19 sounds like the name of a locomotive ("Wreck of Old 97," "Wreck of the 1262," "Wreck of the Number 9"), but Langford meant the nineteenth century: "Industrial Revolution and all that." But in a queer twist of the singer David Thomas's dictum, from an essay on "Wreck of Old 97" and Jan and Dean's "Deadman's Curve," that "what the ballad wants, the ballad gets," a little research turns up the fact that there was a locomotive named the "C-19." A variation on engines that went back to the 1870s, it ran from 1924 through the 1940s for the Denver & Rio Grande Railway. The wreck came in Colorado in 1936, between Kenosha Pass and Denver, killing the engineer, Eugene McGowan, who until Jon Langford came along had never found a place in a song, not that Langford ever heard of him, or had any need to, thanks to the serendipity of the tradition of train-wreck ballads, which will give you a model railroad to play with whether you've asked for it or not, the song taking the shape it wants whatever you think it is you mean to do.

Especially over the last twenty years or so, the music Bob Dylan has made seems to have been based in a hunch that there is a body of American song, a particular ethos of expression, that is a constant. It's a form that in words and musical metaphors, riffs and moans, hesitations and shouts, can always be rediscovered—not revived, with the music deformed according to the needs and demands of the revivalists, but rediscovered whole, speaking as it means to speak—a form that can rediscover and renew whoever remembers it, as if one can not only speak but listen in tongues. In just this sense, throughout Bob Dylan's career—from before he had a career, when he and his high school bandmate John Bucklen were fooling around with Little Richard numbers and making fun of Johnny Cash—people have said the same thing. In Hibbing, Minnesota, in 1958, what Bucklen thought Dylan had taken from someone else he'd written himself; what Bucklen thought was something Dylan had written wasn't. "It doesn't have any sense of being written," Cynthia Gooding said to Dylan on her radio show *Folksingers Choice* in 1962, after Dylan had played his "The Death of Emmett Till." "It sounds as if it just came out of . . . it doesn't have any of those little poetic contortions that mess up so many contemporary ballads." It was all in the presentation, all in the way the song was sung, how it was played, how far the singer could lose himself or herself in the song. Dylan and the members of what would become the Band could be fooling around in a basement near Woodstock in 1967, Dylan would come in with something that Robbie Robertson, the makeshift group's guitarist and sometime drummer, was certain was a folk song; it would turn out to be something Dylan had written the day before. A ballad filled with impossible imagery and winking puns, so clearly written by Dylan drunk on symbolist poetry, would turn out to be three hundred years old. It could be a party in London in 1965, when Donovan sang Dylan's "Mr. Tambourine Man," certain it was an old folk song he'd never heard, and Dylan made D. A. Pennebaker, who was filming that night, turn off his camera. "Most of my songs aren't original," Dylan said to Pennebaker, not happy, caught in his own paradox. "But that one is."

In 1963, Dylan began performing a song called "Seven Curses." The melody, which like the story summoned up feudal England like a magic wand, had to be from one of the oldest British border ballads; according to the folklorist Todd Harvey, who sought its analogue from across the tradition, it was whole cloth. That same year, in an apartment with a tape recorder running, Dylan sang for friends sitting on couches, chairs, and the floor, and "I Rode Out One Morning" came up. No phrase could be more commonplace, more a signal of an ancient ballad—but somehow this isn't really the Scots-Irish "I Roved Out One Morning," and it isn't "As I Went out One Morning," the strange, mystical song, with Thomas Paine hiding in its forest, that would appear on Dylan's album *John Wesley Harding* five years later—in the calculus of the time, which in the world of music was moving very fast in the mid-sixties, a lifetime later. And even if "As I Went out One Morning" is "I Rode Out One Morning," it doesn't matter: to hear one thing as another, to deny that anything can be truly old or really new, is to hear nothing for what it is.

With people coming in and out of the kitchen with new drinks, one-upping each other over who's heard which song first, immediately, with just a sketch of an instrumental theme that is pretty before it's anything else, with the gonging of the bass strings on the guitar pulling back against the easy stroll of the melody, questioning it, nearly a minute of playing before the words "I rode out one morning / For to make me a friend," in the spaces between the notes an enormous sense of suspense and danger is present, and you are somewhere you haven't been before—somewhere, because of the language that is being spoken, anyone can recognize, but where, at bottom, no one has ever quite been before. In the way he takes a step back from the story he's telling, the singer hints that he isn't telling half of what he knows—that the song was made not to reveal but to conceal. You are riveted in place. Dylan's "I'm Not There," from 1967, begins here—so does "Highlands," from thirty years after that, and "Ain't Talkin'," from almost a decade further on.

One night in the summer of 2013, in St. Paul, Dylan sang "Suzie Baby," in 1959 the first single, an original song, by Bobby Vee and the Shadows. Within a year, Bobby Vee would be a huge teen idol living in the Top 10—but in the summer of 1959 the Shadows were just a high school band from Fargo, North Dakota, trying to sound like Buddy Holly. They'd played in public for the first time only months before, when they'd filled in for him in Moorhead, Minnesota, for the date Holly was supposed to have played the day his plane crashed after a show in Clear Lake, Iowa; for a few weeks in the summer of 1959, Bob Dylan, then an eighteen-year-old Robert Zimmerman who had been present in Duluth for Holly's second-to-last show, for the moment calling himself Elston Gunn, joined the Shadows as a piano player.

"Suzie Baby" was well-crafted generic romantic pop—"Suzie baby, where are you?"—and it was singular, a fatalistic slide to an abandonment that felt real. Now in St. Paul, more than half a century after he'd first played the song, with Vee himself, now fading from Alzheimer's disease but capable of enthusiasm and joy, present in the crowd, Dylan sang "Suzie Baby" as a commonplace rock 'n' roll folk song—a song seemingly written more by its style than by any actual person, a song heard and received that way, and yet a field for individuality, for subjectivity and art. "I've played all over the world," Dylan said, echoing the folk-lyric line that in the nineteenth century began to jump from song to song, *I've been all around the world, boys,* "with everyone from Mick Jagger to Madonna. I've been on the stage with most of those people," Dylan said musically. "But the most beautiful"—or he might have said "meaningful"—"person I've been on the stage with is a man who's here tonight, who used to sing a song called 'Suzie Baby.' I want to say, Bobby Vee is actually here tonight." With border-town guitar underlying every phrase, the tune came forth so delicately, suspended in time, as if Dylan, walking on eggshells and not cracking a single one, was glancing back to the past not from the present moment but from well in the future, where with Bobby Vee dead, Bob Dylan dead, the old folk song was still sung. As it was played that night, it could almost have been a pre–Civil War parlor tune, composed and copyrighted and by the end of the nineteenth century folded into the commonplace of a million front-room pianos, whoever wrote the song as forgotten as if he'd never been born. Without question it's a song that could have been made by anyone in the last sixty years, a song that did not refer back to the Buddy Holly of 1957 or in its moment to the Bobby Vee of 1959 or forward to the Bob Dylan of 2013, but includes, subsumes, and erases each date in turn. And this is where we find "Ballad of Hollis Brown"—or where Dylan found it.

"Ballad of Hollis Brown" feels plainly like a song from the Great Depression. That was how John Henry Faulk positioned it in his show—he or his producers might have taken it not as a new song but as an old one. If you look at the YouTube videos people have made to illustrate the song, of Dylan's recording or versions by a dozen other people, the Dust Bowl is everywhere. But the song could as well be straight out of Michael Lesy's *Wisconsin Death Trip,* his found chronicle of the devastation the depression of the 1890s brought to farm communities like Black River Falls, when social life came apart under the pressure of the collapse of the commodities market, drought, epidemics of childhood disease, arson, tramp armies that stripped towns and farms like locusts, and the waves of insanity, suicide, and murder rolling through the small towns where everybody knew everybody else. "By the end of the nineteenth century," Lesy wrote in 1973, amazed that the terror he had uncovered had been completely forgotten, that the events he followed had somehow never entered the American imagination, or had been banished from it, "country towns had become charnel houses and the counties that surrounded them had become places of dry bones. The land and its farms were filled with the guilty voices of women mourning for their children and the aimless mutterings of men asking about jobs."

"Henry Johnson, an old bachelor of Grand Dyke," the editors of the *Badger State Banner,* Frank and George Cooper, wrote in April 1891, in one of scores of local news items Lesy spread across his pages in a litany that turned into a traditional murder ballad like "Tom Dooley" and then into *The Last House on the Left,* "cut off the heads of all his hens recently, made a bonfire of his best clothes, and killed himself with arsenic." "Mrs. John Larson, wife of a farmer living in the town of Troy," the editors wrote three months later, "drowned her three children in Lake St. Croix during a fit of insanity. Her husband, on finding her absent from the house, began a search and found her at the lake shore . . . two of her children lying in the sand dead. The third could not be found. Mrs. Larson imagines that devils pursue her."

"Ballad of Hollis Brown" comes off of *The Times They Are A-Changin'* as the present day, a news story, and yet for so many it has always seemed to be set in the past—in the completely historicized, even romanticized past, where people listening to the song are protected from any implication in its drama—because in America poverty is so easily turned into art. That is because to educated, worldly people, the poor as they are captured in representations—whether, during the Great Depression, in the FSA photographs of Wolcott, Walker Evans, Dorothea Lange, and Ben Shahn, or in the paintings and

woodcuts of Thomas Hart Benton and Rock-
well Kent, or in the commercial recordings of
commonplace songs made in the 1920s and '30s
and collected in 1952 by the folklorist Harry
Smith on an anthology he at first called simply
American Folk Music, or in the way that the educated project representations of the poor, who,
having been fetishized in American art since the
nineteenth century, and, having thus been given
designated roles in the picture America draws of
itself, project representations upon themselves—
seem like art because they appear archaic, like
survivals of a past civilization, artifacts more than
people. They take on the aura that, as explored
by the Surrealists in the 1920s, old buildings can
possess: something that in its own time was
ordinary, workaday, seemingly made without
desire, can generations later appear alive with
idiosyncrasy, style, even hidden meaning, as the
eye becomes attuned to tiny details and oddities
that were secreted in the building, to set it
apart, to be discovered after the artist—not the
architect, with his degrees and his awards, but
the mason, the carpenter, the welder—has been
forgotten. And this is true not only when we
look back at, say, Walker Evans's photographs
made in Hale County, Alabama, in 1936, but as

we are brought back to pay attention to his hand, his eye, his time.

The people we are looking at, that Evans is looking at, dressed in feed bags, the faces of women in their twenties and thirties looking not merely fifty or even sixty, but out of time as we measure it, do not live in the United States as it was understood then, or as it is understood now. Where do they live? They live in representations. When Harry Smith assembled his anthology, he chose for a cover a mystical work by the sixteenth-century engraver Theodore de Bry that showed the hand of God tuning a one-stringed instrument called a celestial monochord; when the set was reissued in the early 1960s, Folkways, Smith's record company, with roots in the Popular Front, chose a new cover, a 1930s Ben Shahn photo of a starving farmer, the life gone out of his eyes, perfectly congruent with the ideology of the folk revival as portrayed on television by John Henry Faulk—a picture of a man that by 1964 any well-versed folk musician could have easily translated as Hollis Brown. And, looking at his copy of the Smith anthology, Dylan himself might have made the same translation. "In times behind, I too / wished I'd lived in the hungry thirties /

an' blew in like Woody / t' New York City / an'
sang for dimes / on subway trains," Dylan wrote
in his liner notes to *The Times They Are A-Changin'*.
How do you get from that cheap romanticism
to the plainness of "Hollis Brown"?

The story of the song is the story of how Bob
Dylan was able to make the song sing as if it were
not his, as if it were as found as the images
Michael Lesy discovered in the files of Charles
Van Schaick, in the 1890s the town photogra-
pher of Black River Falls, Wisconsin—most un-
forgettably, in a posed family portrait, the eyes
of a dark-haired young woman burning with
hate, with the promise that she'll kill anyone
who dares to look at her. It's the story of how
Dylan finally made the song slip its skin, until it
could feel as common as "The Coo Coo Bird,"
as mythical as "Frankie and Johnny," as factual
as "Casey Jones."

"I don't sorta run around and do with the
newspapers like a lot of people do—spread newspapers all around—and pick something up to
write a song about," Dylan said to Pete Seeger
on a radio show in 1962. Even though it is a
writer imagining himself into the life of a person
he has made up, "Hollis Brown" sounded like a
news item ("Community shocked after man kills

family, self," one could have read in the local newspaper in San Carlos Park, Florida, on June 10, 2014: "Investigators say the family did not have a history with law enforcement, nor did they have any contact with the Department of Children and Families"), but it wasn't; it wasn't that simple. "I don't even consider that I wrote it when I get it done," Dylan said of his songs. "The song was there before me, before I came along. I just sorta came down and I sorta took it down with a pencil . . . That's how I feel about it."

Dylan hung his words on the frame and the melody of the murder ballad "Pretty Polly." In 2012, in Oxford, Mississippi, a band called Chauncey and the Beast combined the two songs, the singer Lady Tiffany alternating "Pretty Polly" verses—"Pretty Polly, pretty Polly, come take a walk with me"—with the guitarist Chauncey Mauney's from "Hollis Brown." As Dylan did, they followed the version of "Pretty Polly" the Virginia mountaineer Dock Boggs recorded in 1927, but the full force of Boggs's coolly psychopathic, relentlessly syncopated banjo-driven performance did not emerge in Dylan's song right away. In its British beginnings, the man who kills and buries Polly has a clear motive: she's pregnant. In American versions, the pregnancy has disappeared, and there is no motive at all—because of the Puritan shadow, or because singers tapped into the Gothic strain in what D. H. Lawrence called the American subterranean from the beginning— and that made the song far more terrifying, because there was no motive beyond the pure desire to kill.

"In August 1962, Bob was in the audience at Gerde's Folk City (a folk-oriented night club) in New York City where I was playing for a couple of weeks," the folk revivalist Mike Seeger of the New Lost City Ramblers wrote in 1994. ("The supreme archetype," Dylan called Seeger in his book *Chronicles, Volume One,* in 2004: "he had come to purify the church.") "I asked him to join me at the end of my set." Dylan performed "Ballad of Hollis Brown"; Seeger backed him on banjo. It would have been one of the first times Dylan sang the song in public, if not the first, and it was a turning point. Mike Seeger was the keeper of the keys; he played the old songs that everyone in the folk world played, Dylan included, "as good as it was possible to play them," Dylan wrote. "The thought occurred to me that maybe I'd have to write my own folk songs, ones that Mike didn't know." "Ballad of Hollis Brown" was one of the first, but it was also an alchemist's song—as Dylan sang it that night, it could have been heard by those in the audience as a song that had always been there, a song that Mike Seeger had handed down to Bob Dylan, not the other way around. And as the first recorded version of the song can make you think, Dylan had yet to feel his way into the song he'd been given.

When Dylan performed "Ballad of Hollis Brown" at a hootenanny at the Carnegie Chapter Hall in September, a month after he'd sung the song with Seeger, there is no sense of event. There are lines Dylan would keep over many performances: "There's bedbugs on your baby's bed, there's chinches on your wife / Gangrene snuck inside, cutting you like a knife." It was too much—why not the plague? The unusual structure of the song, really the mind of the song—the first two couplets of a verse repeated once, the third sealing them both like a gravedigger shoveling dirt into a hole, the structure of "Pretty Polly," but also of the blues, the sinister force of the singer addressing Hollis Brown directly, always "You look for work and money," "Your eyes fix on the shotgun," *you you you,* not the third-person address anyone else would use, the voice at once accusatory and empathetic, the prosecutor and the psychiatrist in the same breath—has no definition.

Perhaps a month later, at the Gaslight Café, a small Greenwich Village basement club on Mac-Dougal Street, the picture comes into focus instantly, so darkly that in your imagination you can barely make out the faces of the people in the song. Each string seems to vibrate alone, without hearing any other. There are hints of melodies from other songs, creeping in and out of the slow pulse of the music—nothing is rushed. But the singing is slack. Dylan drags against his own music, falling behind it, at times whooping to keep your ear, as if he knows his fingers are writing a check his voice can't cash.

"This is 'The Rise and Fall of Hollis Brown,'" Dylan says in December of the same year, making a clackety, banjo-like demo recording for his music publisher. "It's a true story." It wasn't true—not newspaper true—and this day it isn't emotionally or morally true either. The story doesn't come true as it's sung and played. Perhaps a month earlier, Dylan recorded a version of the song meant for his second album, *The Freewheelin' Bob Dylan,* and there was nothing there at all.

The performance is hollow: the arrangement is loose, the voice is hectoring, the language in Dylan's tone of voice is purely that of the protest song. "Bob Dylan wrote propaganda songs!" Mike Watt of the San Pedro punk band the Minutemen shouted more than twenty years later. The propaganda singer sees evil in the world and dares you to see what he sees—implicitly the singer flatters you, gathering you to his side, so that together you can face the world as it is, and with a pure heart. But if, in a performance, you hear not only the singer but the song itself thinking, here the song doesn't think. "You ain't got no money, boy," Dylan sings, and the character that's taking shape drops right out of the song. For "Is there anyone that cares," Dylan gives the words a sarcastic shudder, saying, *I care, I wrote the song,* but no one else does. There is no suspense, no horror. With "seven breezes blowing," Dylan seems afraid of the line. He can't give it weight, he can't pull the trigger—and seconds later, for "There's seven people dead / On a South Dakota farm," he's giving a speech. *There is a* farm *problem; we need a new farm* policy. *I have introduced a bill that*— The song is left off the album.

In the summer of 1963, for *The Times They Are A-Changin'*, Dylan recorded the song again. This was his full-out protest album, his conscience-of-a-generation album, and unlike almost any other Bob Dylan album before or since, it was completely humorless. "May God us keep from Single Vision & Newton's Sleep," Blake wrote in 1802; this album created the single idea that makes a hero in modern media. For Bob Dylan it fixed the identity, or the mask, that for so many who thrilled to it could never be altered in any way, not without a sense of betrayal and shame. With *The Times They Are A-Changin'* Bob Dylan would build a prison of fame and righteousness that he would spend the next years, even the next decades, trying to escape, and for some in his audience that prison will always be a castle he can never be permitted to escape. But for this recording, the song escaped it.

What is happening in the song is happening as you listen—the sense of event is overpowering, even as the event pieces itself together out of sidelong glances, subtle gestures, barely uttered words. For a small farmer, the Depression is always present, a scourge that might be only a season away, the disaster that can come at any

time; now it has. As in the Band's "King Harvest (Has Surely Come)," with its burning barn
and mad horse, with the desperation in Richard
Manuel's "Just don't judge me by my shoes!"
opening the door to murder or suicide, this is the
pastoral; this is ordinary life. The steady strumming from the Faulk show has disappeared into
harsh, bright picking, the strings themselves
speaking, arguing, throwing stones at each other.
The measured urgency in the music is like a
curse, precisely because that urgency is measured,
controlled, handed down by some malevolent
force—a force like God, or justice, or money.
The cadence of the singing is even more defined,
the first lines of a verse bitten off, the words
of the last line tumbling after each other like
balls in a chute, each line making you afraid of
whatever line it is that will come next, until
with "Your baby's a-cryin' louder now, it's
pounding on your brain / Your baby's a-cryin'
louder now, it's pounding on your brain," you feel
not what the singer is feeling, but what the character is feeling, but he is no longer a character.
"I was beginning to feel like a character from
within these songs," Dylan would write in
Chronicles of the old ballads he was learning from
folk musicians in Minneapolis, before he ever set

foot in New York, "even beginning to think like one," and here he has performed that transference on the listener. Someone who says his name is Hollis Brown is standing before you, holding out his hand.

The melody rings. As Dylan sings, despite the slashing in his delivery, so strong you can picture the song sung by a sword, everything is understated. There is no sense of authorship, and no audience. The singer does not determine the action; Hollis Brown does. The singer doesn't judge, because he is not an actor in the drama. As the song goes on, behind the inexorable, unbreakable fatalism of the main theme on the guitar, notes begin to ping. They seem higher every time, the story in the song protesting against itself, each ping a *no* that is swept up and then swept away with the *bum-bum, bum-bum* that rules the music. What is about to happen has already happened, because it has happened thousands of times before—as Michael Lesy writes, in the 1890s parents killed their children because in a world utterly out of control, it was one act they could take to determine fate before they were buried by it—and it will happen thousands of times in the future, from South Dakota to San Carlos Park, from California to the New York Island. What is about to happen hasn't happened yet, because there is no past and there is no future, there is only the unfolding moment, where Hollis Brown stands frozen by choice, and anything is possible. It is one of those songs that, every time you hear it, you hope, you force yourself to believe, that it will all come out differently.

With that performance, the song walked away from Bob Dylan and into the world, as if it had always been there, which it had. Bob Dylan found it as surely as Michael Lesy found deathly eyes in a family portrait. Both changed what they found, added highlights, cut away anything that would clutter the story they heard, but neither family portrait—the one in *Wisconsin Death Trip,* the one in "Ballad of Hollis Brown"— belonged to either of them, any more than "Stagger Lee" or "Frankie and Johnny" belonged to Bill Dooley.

In 1895, in St. Louis, a man called "Stag" Lee Shelton shot and killed a man named Billy Lyons; that real event, covered in the newspapers, turned into the ballad first known as "Stagolee Shot Billy." In 1899, in the same city, a woman named Frankie Baker shot and killed a man named Allen Britt; that real event, also reported in the press, turned into the ballad "Frankie Killed Allen," which became "Frankie and Albert" and then "Frankie and Johnny." There have been hundreds of versions of these songs in countless variations. They were likely already circulating before Lee Shelton and Frankie Baker went to trial, and yet, by the 1920s if not before, the real events had been swallowed up by myth, and the real actors, as authors of their own lives, of their own songs, had ceased to exist.

The stories and the songs had become common property—but the folklorist Cecil Brown makes a powerful argument that both songs, formed in such a manner that neither would ever lose its essential shape, that each would resist whatever deformations the future would find it appealing to inflict on it, were composed on the spot by a street singer and ballad hawker named Bill Dooley, who soon enough walked off the St. Louis stage to an unknown fate. Bob Dylan wrote "Ballad of Hollis Brown," but he also found it—and which greater, to be remembered and celebrated, or to put something into the world so vivid and complete that we can't imagine the world, in this case the world of American song and story, without it, to have transformed an everyday event that did not happen into one that did, and then disappear, unless the right word is really escape?

"Ballad of Hollis Brown" is three songs: Bob Dylan's song; the folk song; and his song that sounds like a folk song, authorless, written by history and weather, no original and no copy. And it's the last formation of the song that hits. "The Heart is the Capital of the Mind," Emily Dickinson wrote:

> The Mind is a single State—
> The Heart and the Mind together make
> A single Continent—
> One—is the Population—
> Numerous enough—
> This ecstatic Nation
> Seek—it is Yourself.

In "Ballad of Hollis Brown" it is a nation emerging out of D. H. Lawrence's offhand judgment, calling Hollis Brown and Clint Eastwood into being well in advance, that the "essential American soul is hard, isolate, stoic, and a killer," a nation made of isolation but also friendship, even in its absence an absolute value. It is a nation where the prospect of violence is the absolute so-

lution to absolute problems; it is a nation of abso-
lutes. In this nation, who is the one who makes
it? It is the character; it is the tale-teller; it's the
listener. Each at any moment, in a shifting dance,
imagining himself or herself the other.

Other people took up the song—most memo-
rably, at the start, Nina Simone, who made it a
centerpiece, or a black hole, in concerts in 1965.
("That she was recording my songs," Dylan said
in 2015, "validated everything that I was about.")
In 1975 Leon Russell opened it as if it were a
slavery-time ring shout. In the 1990s and after it
reappeared everywhere, like a common repressed
memory. There were fierce recordings by Stephen Stills of Crosby, Stills & Nash—what he
couldn't say as a singer he said as a guitarist—and
the British writer and singer Billy Childish, who
reimagined the song as a variant of Them's
"Mystic Eyes." There were live performances by
the grandiose Chicago punk band Rise Again,
who transformed detail into cliché, by the heavy-
metal band Nazareth, put to shame with an
anarchic attack by the Swedish death-metal band
Entombed. But the most unsettling reading came
in the early 1970s, in a Stooges rehearsal. With

Iggy Pop wailing in the background, trying out the chords and the words of the song as if he were trying on clothes, looking for the right sound, the right tone of voice, teaching himself the song as the drummer Scott Asheton and the bassist Ron Asheton made a stark, unchanging pulse that still kept "Pretty Polly" alive in the rhythm, the story being told was altogether from the guitarist James Williamson. He came out of the music like an avenger, a nightmare, a killer, Hollis Brown as Richard Speck, the twisting lines he snaked through the song slow, patient, watching as life set everyone in the song up for death. It was frightening; it made perfect sense that one of the fan videos put on YouTube simply let the performance orchestrate footage from a Soviet film about the siege of Stalingrad. And of Dylan's own performances as the years went on—for the worldwide telecast of the 1985 Live Aid benefit to combat famine in Africa, in terrible makeup, presumably offering "Hollis Brown" as a treatise on hunger, playing with Ron Wood and Keith Richards, who looked just as bad, the song was a mess, and horribly powerful, not a treatise on anything, but a story happening as you watched—perhaps the most memorable was a recording made in 1993, with Mike Seeger on banjo, for Seeger's so-called Third Annual Farewell Reunion.

The banjo at once pushes the music and adds a sense of reflection. Dylan's vocal is distant, as if this truly is an old folk song, it's been sung forever, everyone knows the story, and that's the point. There's nothing new under the sun, but by saying exactly that, again and again, in the difference in inflection each time the thing is said, something you didn't know, that you never heard before, changes the landscape of the song. That "Pretty Polly" rhythm, taking the story past the realm of fatalism, into the preordained, makes a setting where the slightest shift in manner can feel like a ricochet. Dylan's slow, sliding tone of voice could not be more different from the direct, engaged, factual approach he applied to the traditional blues and folk songs he was recording at the same time for his albums *Good as I Been to You* and *World Gone Wrong*. The drama comes when he rises out of the seen-it-all-before with a stress of surprise or offense, and then goes back to the story as if it's a weather report, which of course it partly is.

Today there is a four-piece band from Brooklyn called Hollis Brown that did not include the song on their first album—they didn't have to. The name gave them something to live up to, and they did. People continue to test themselves against the song. The filmmaker David Lynch's version, from 2013—based, he said, not on Bob Dylan's recording at all, but on Nina Simone's—is deathly slow, because of the weight that burdens it. Lynch's guitar is thick, impenetrable, a moving wall. You can't imagine anything breaking through it—and from the moment Lynch opens his mouth and in his crazy-old-man voice says the first two words, *Hollis Brown*, you know you're hearing the story of a real person. "Why did you decide to tackle Bob Dylan's 'The Ballad of Hollis Brown'?" he was asked. He and his producer, Lynch said, played back a sequence of the album: "We both felt like something was missing, and then we remembered that we didn't play that song. I think it's a very important texture for the album, number one, and number two, with the financial crises and people out of work and hard up for money, I think it's a very timely song."

"It's a true story," said the person who took it down with a pencil.

NOTES

Folk Songs and More Folk Songs! Westinghouse Broadcasting Company. Recorded March 4, 1963; broadcast in May 1963. Produced by Michael R. Santangelo, directed by Jack Kuney, written by Robert Ruthman and Douglas Watt, drawings and design by Ed Renfro. Dylan's performances of "Blowin' in the Wind," "Man of Constant Sorrow," and "Ballad of Hollis Brown" can be found on *Bob Dylan: The Genuine Telecasts 1963–2002* (Scorpio Video Archives). "Man of Constant Sorrow" is also included on Dylan's *No Direction Home: The Soundtrack—The Bootleg Series Vol. 7* (Columbia Legacy, 2005). Full show courtesy Michael Goldberg.

Marion Post Wolcott, *Lame Deer (vicinity), Montana. Skull in front of Indian steam bath on Cheyenne Indian Tongue River Reservation to keep evil spirits away, a belief which is part of their "medicine,"* August 1941, a Farm Security Administration work now in the Library of Congress.

Bob Dylan, "Gates of Hate," unrecorded, published in *Sing Out!* (October/November 1962). Cited in Clinton Heylin, *Revolution in the Air: The Songs of Bob Dylan, 1957–1973* (Chicago: Chicago Review Press, 2009), 92. The folk singer Phil Ochs's tendentious "The Ballad of John Henry Faulk," probably written about the same time as Dylan's song and recorded for *Broadside* magazine, was released on Ochs's *The Broadside Tapes 1* (Smithsonian Folkways, 1989/1995).

Bob Dylan, "It just went through me." Robert Love, "Bob Dylan: The Uncut Interview." *AARP The Magazine* (February/March 2015).

Mavis Staples, "My lost love." See Graham Rockingham, "Mavis Staples recalls her lost love," *Hamilton Spectator,* January 21, 2012.

Mavis Staples, "It was always in my mind." See Greg Kot, *I'll Take You There: Mavis Staples, the Staple Singers, and the March Up Freedom's Highway* (New York: Scribner, 2014), 88–89.

Bob Dylan and Mavis Staples, "Gonna Change My Way of Thinking" (with "I'm Gonna Sit at the Welcome Table"), from *Gotta Serve Somebody: The Gospel Songs of Bob Dylan—Performed by Shirley Caesar, Lee Williams & the Spiritual QC's, Dottie Peoples, Fairfield Four, Sounds of Blackness, Aaron Neville, Helen Bayer, Chicago Mass Choir, Mighty Clouds of Joy, Rance Allen* (Columbia, 2003).

Bob Dylan, "This Land Is Your Land," Carnegie Chapter Hall, November 4, 1961, included on *No Direction Home: The Soundtrack—The Bootleg Series, Vol. 7* (Columbia, 2005). It was used as closing music for the Acting Company's 2012–2013 production of *John Steinbeck's Of Mice and Men,* directed by Ian Belknap.

Bob Dylan, "Ballad of Hollis Brown," *The Times They Are A-Changin',* recorded August 7, 1963 (Columbia, 1964).

Jon Langford, "Lost in America," first performed May 16, 2003, in Portland, Oregon, as part of the *This American Life* road show "Lost in America," and first broadcast on *This American Life* June 6, 2003. Recorded for Langford's *Goldbrick* (ROIR, 2006). A devastating performance can be found on YouTube as "Jon Langford's Ship and Pilot—Tractor Tavern—April 15, 2006."

Jon Langford, "The Industrial Revolution." "I don't think I really wrote that song anyway," Langford says. "Like most of them it just fell out with a thud." E-mail to GM, August 13, 2013.

David Thomas, "What the ballad wants." From "Destiny in My Right Hand: 'The Wreck of Old 97' and 'Dead Man's Curve,'" in *The Rose & the Briar: Death, Love and Liberty in the American Ballad,* ed. Sean Wilentz and Greil Marcus (New York: Norton, 2005), 165. An indelible rendition of "Wreck of Old 97" by John Mellencamp can be found on *The Rose & the Briar* soundtrack album (Columbia, 2005).

Jeff Johnson, "C19 Locomotive History: The Colorado Classic," blackstonemodels.com.

Inflection

John Bucklen, in *Tales of Rock and Roll Part Four: Highway 61 Revisited,* directed by James Marsh (BBC Arena, 1993).

Robbie Robertson, conversation with GM, 1996.

Bob Dylan, "Most of my songs aren't original." D. A. Pennebaker, conversation with GM, 2011.

"Seven Curses," as an outtake from *The Times They Are A-Changin',* recorded August 6, 1963, included on *The Bootleg Series Vols. 1-3 (Rare & Unreleased) 1961–1991* (Columbia 1993), and as a more striking live performance from Carnegie Hall, April 12, 1963, on an officially prepared but then withdrawn live album, *Bob Dylan in Concert* (bootleg).

Todd Harvey, *The Formative Dylan: Transmission and Stylistic Influences, 1961–1963* (Lanham, MD: Scarecrow Press, 2001), 97.

"I Rode Out One Morning," from "Second McKenzie Tape," April 12, 1963, on *I Was So Much Younger Then,* CD 3, #21 (Dandelion bootleg).

"Suzie Baby," as performed at Midway Stadium, St. Paul, Minnesota, July 10, 2013. See Corey Anderson, "Audio: Bob Dylan performing Bobby Vee's 'Suzie Baby' at Midway Stadium," minnpost.com. One attendee described the setting as "Totally midwestern—when 'All Along the Watchtower' began, the train running past the stadium blew three perfect whistles."

Michael Lesy, *Wisconsin Death Trip* (Albuquerque: University of New Mexico Press, 2000 [1973]), n.p.

American Folk Music, comp. Harry Smith (Folkways, 1952); *Anthology of American Folk Music* (Folkways, 1958).

Bob Dylan, "In times too." From "11 Outlined Epitaphs," notes to *The Times They Are A-Changin'.*

Bob Dylan, "I don't sorta run around." Pete Seeger with Bob Dylan, *Broadside Show,* WBAI-FM, New York City, May 1962. Courtesy Jeff Rosen.

Chauncey and the Beast featuring Lady Tiffany, "Pretty Polly"/"Hollis Brown," at the Snackbar, Oxford, Mississippi, January 4, 2012, YouTube.

Dock Boggs, "Pretty Polly," originally issued by Brunswick, 1927, on *Country Blues* (Revenant, 1997).

Mike Seeger, "In August 1962." From Seeger's notes to his *Third Annual Farewell Reunion* (Rounder, 1994), which also included collaborations with Maria Muldaur, Olabelle and David Reed, Ralph Stanley, Jean Ritchie, Jimmie Driftwood, Hazel Dickens, Peggy Seeger, a reunion of the New Lost City Ramblers with John Cohen and Tracy Schwarz, a stunning "Cripple Creek" with Etta Baker, and more. "I strive for really traditional-feeling sounds," Seeger wrote, "some of which may have never existed before."

Bob Dylan on Mike Seeger. Bob Dylan, *Chronicles, Volume One* (New York: Simon and Schuster, 2004), 69–70, 71.

Bob Dylan, "Ballad of Hollis Brown," as performed at Carnegie Chapter Hall, September 22, 1962, included on *The 50th Anniversary Collection,* CD #4, track #4 (Columbia, 2013).

Bob Dylan, "Ballad of Hollis Brown," as performed at the Gaslight Café, c. October 1962, included on *The Second Gaslight Tape* (Wild Wolf bootleg), and on *The 50th Anniversary Collection,* CD #4, track #11.

Bob Dylan, "Ballad of Hollis Brown," as included on *The Witmark Demos: 1962–1964—The Bootleg Series, Vol. 9* (Columbia, 2010).

Bob Dylan, "Ballad of Hollis Brown," as recorded for *The Freewheelin' Bob Dylan,* probably November 14, 1963, included on *The 50th Anniversary Collection,* CD #2, track #17, take two, and on *Walk Like a Duck Stink Like a Skunk* (Snowball bootleg).

The Band, "King Harvest (Has Surely Come)," *The Band* (Capitol, 1969).

Bob Dylan, "I was beginning to feel." Dylan, *Chronicles, Volume One,* 240.

Cecil Brown, on Bill Dooley and "Stag" Lee Shelton, in *Stagolee Shot Billy* (Cambridge, MA: Harvard University Press, 2004). On Dooley and Frankie Baker, see Brown's "We Did Them Wrong: The Ballad of Frankie and Albert," in *The Rose & the Briar,* 142–145.

Emily Dickinson, "The Heart is the Capital of the Mind," *The Poems of Emily Dickinson,* ed. R. W. Franklin (Cambridge, MA: Belknap Press, 1999).

Bob Dylan, "That she was recording." Acceptance speech at MusiCares Person of the Year Awards, February 5, 2015.

Iggy and the Stooges, "Ballad of Hollis Brown," included on *Wild Love—The Detroit Rehearsals and More* (Bomp, 2001).

Bob Dylan and Mike Seeger, "Ballad of Hollis Brown," included on Mike Seeger, *Third Annual Farewell Reunion.*

Hollis Brown, *Ride on the Train* (Alive/Natural Sound, 2013).

David Lynch, "Ballad of Hollis Brown," *The Big Dream* (Sacred Bones, 2013).

David Lynch, "Why did you decide." From "Sometimes It's Very Good to Go Back and Revisit Old Work," interview with Stephen Deusner, *Salon,* August 6, 2013.

Disappearance and Forgetting
"Last Kind Words Blues," Geeshie Wiley

In 2006, Mississippi Records, a small label in Portland, Oregon, put out a collection of blues and gospel 78s by storied performers—Blind Willie and Kate McTell, Robert Wilkins, the Mississippi Moaner, Cannon's Jug Stompers—on an LP called *Last Kind Words 1926–1953*.

The sleeve is a front-and-back cartoon, a colorful folk-art grid of a pleasant, sunny, orderly American place, full of people going from here to there, looking out the window, and, in crude little speech balloons, what they're saying and thinking. On the back cover, there's a neighborhood of apartment houses. "I AM LIKE SOME KIND OF LOG ROLLING," says a man. "DING DONG," says a man facing him from halfway down the block. "THATS OK," says someone else, "IS IT A FISH I DON'T KNOW WHAT THE HELLS GOING ON ANYMORE." The dialogue, seemingly addressed to no one, begins to accumulate. Here and there you can catch what might be pieces of a song: "IT IS HARD TO LEAVE YOU." "DEATH IS ONLY A DREAM." "EVERYWHERE IS COLD." "IT WAS SO CARELESS SO VERY CARELESS." "IM GOING." "I SEE YOU."

Turn the sleeve over and you're downtown. There are broad streets, a tree every half block or so, a few more cars than that, about the same number of people on the street as cars. "THAT IS NO WAY TO GET ALONG NOW," one man says to another. They are the only people even acknowledging the presence of anyone else. People are talking to themselves, or to the air: "DONT LET NOBODY TURN YOU AROUND." "MONEY CANT BUY YOUR SOUL." "SALVATION." "NO KIND WORDS NOWHERE." "DEATH IS ONLY A DREAM." It's a portrait of nearly complete isolation (a woman talking on the phone saying "I CALLED YOU THIS MORNING" might be speaking to an actual person, or leaving a message). Each phrase is its own kind of last word, with no sense that anyone is listening.

The first song on the collection is the only one that lives up to the cover art, probably because the song inspired it: "Last Kind Words Blues," from 1930, issued under the name of a singer and guitarist called Geeshie Wiley. It was one of only six songs she recorded, all at the same session in Grafton, Wisconsin, for the Paramount label, a division of the Wisconsin Chair Company. It was a rational business model: furniture companies made expensive phonograph cabinets, a prestige item, and then they made records for people to play on them. Founded in 1917, recording everything from cocktail jazz to standards to polkas to marches to Ethel Waters's "That Dada Strain" ("Have you heard it / Have you heard it . . . It will shake you/ It will make you / Go insane"—Tristan Tzara was thrilled), by 1926 Paramount had become a race label. It made records by and marketed to African-Americans, especially in stores in the South, but also by salesmen going door-to-door, through ads in the *Chicago Defender,* in shops on the South Side, in Detroit and Harlem, and even at the hands of Pullman porters. Paramount sold hundreds of thousands of copies of records by Blind Lemon Jefferson, among them songs that from his day to ours have never been out of mind: "Matchbox Blues," "Easy Rider Blues," "Black Snake Moan," "Jack O'Diamonds," "Chinch Bug Blues."

Over the next years Paramount, with scouts in the South funneling performers by train to Chicago and then to Wisconsin, would record almost all of the singers who today stand as giants in the schools of Mississippi Delta blues, and as performers who, if left out of any conversation about American art, would leave that conversation incomplete, if not a fraud: Charley Patton, Tommy Johnson, Son House, Willie Brown, Skip James, and far more. Victor was paying Al Jolson $10,000 to record a single song; Paramount could make money paying a singer fifty to seventy-five dollars for each side of a 78, with no royalties and no publishing rights.

Sometimes, as with Charley Patton, the company would press tens of thousands of copies of a release, sometimes a thousand or less, but in all cases the commitment to quality was the same. Paramount was famous for making the worst-sounding records on the market. In the 1950s and '60s, collectors of those few Skip James or Son House records that had survived—sometimes only a single copy—used to joke that Paramounts sounded so bad they must have been made out of dirt. They were made out of dirt: lamp blacking, shellac, cotton filling, and clay from the banks of the Milwaukee River, which ran right by the Paramount factory in Grafton. Workers would leave defective records in stacks outside the plant; along with local schoolchildren, they'd sail them out into the river, where Skip James's "Devil Got My Woman" raced Son House's "My Black Mama" to Lake Michigan.

Like the five other recordings Geeshie Wiley made under her own name or that of her musical partner, the singer and guitarist L.V. Thomas (that was her whole, real name, which was rendered on Paramount labels as Elvie Thomas)—"Skinny Leg Blues," "Motherless Child Blues," "Over to My House," "Pick Poor Robin Clean," and "Eagles on a Half"—"Last Kind Words Blues," as one writer has said, "rests on a bed of static." But it is not just noise. The difference is that the static, the sound of the Milwaukee River, is inseparable, now, from the voice of the song. It drapes an aura of the faraway, the lost, and the abandoned over the performance, and the performance was all of those things from the start. The static—"that makes you feel as though the song might disappear into the ether at any moment"—speaks a language in which even the most clearly voiced word is ambiguous in its setting, and the setting itself is visible only through its own haze.

It is appropriate: until the publication in 2014 of John Jeremiah Sullivan's "The Ballad of Geeshie and Elvie" in the *New York Times Magazine,* nobody really knew anything about Geeshie Wiley and Elvie Thomas. Though blues fanatics searched for decades, nothing was found: not their real names, not where and when they were born, where they were from, where they lived, or when, presumably, they died. With one exception: in 1961, the blues scholar Mack McCormick of Houston, pursuing the idea that the truest source of the blues was Texas, not Mississippi, located Thomas, right there in the same city. He'd followed the notion that "Elvie" was likely a corruption of L.V.—it was not uncommon for women of her generation to be named with letters. Though Thomas had long since put aside blues for the church, she talked to McCormick. She gave him the Rosetta stone of what would, half a century later, become Sullivan's quest— but until Sullivan gained access to McCormick's interview transcripts, not a word of what McCormick found circulated anywhere. Sullivan was able to fill in the facts and even the under-currents of Thomas's long life, to the point of convening a reunion of friends, parishioners, and relatives who brought her so close it was maddening she was not there: stories of Thomas as a devout and beloved sister of the church, a powerful gospel singer, a woman one did not approach lightly, a lesbian who always carried a long-barreled pistol under her apron. "Sister L.V. Thomas's voice was, like, melodic," Sister Idell Murray of Mt. Pleasant Missionary Baptist told Sullivan in 2013. "It would just get in your ears, and it would just float . . . I remember once thinking about the slaves, when they were out working and singing. That was the type [of] images that you would get from her music, because it would just carry you away." But while as Thomas spoke to McCormick Wiley came half into focus, at least for the first part of her life, for the rest she returned to the mist.

From McCormick's typescripts, which were found by Caitlin Rose Love, a researcher Sullivan had put together with McCormick, Sullivan learned that Elvie was L.V.; that she was born in 1891 in Houston; that Geeshie Wiley's given name was Lillie Mae. Thomas began playing guitar when she was eleven, in about 1902. "There were blues even back then," she said to McCormick—which meant she remembered when there wasn't.★ Through census and county records, Thomas's unpublished words led Sullivan to Wiley's birth year, 1908, and to her arrest, in 1931, for the murder of her second husband, with a knife—but not what happened after that, or, really, what happened. She might have run; she might have gone to prison; the case might never have been prosecuted. It was Houston, it was 1931, it was two black people, and who cared? After that, except for Thomas's mention to McCormick that in the mid-thirties Wiley was in Oklahoma, that she "was supposed to be" in West Texas in the mid-fifties, nothing.

Thomas was seventeen years older than Wiley, making them unusual partners; Thomas was thirty-eight when they recorded, Wiley twenty-one or twenty-two. She gave Wiley her name, Thomas told McCormick, which Para-

---

★ "I can't hardly name them," she told McCormick. "I don't know that those songs had a name . . . One song was 'Oh, My Babe Take Me Back' and another was 'Jack o' Diamonds.' There was a lot of set-pieces, stuff that'd be called for dancing, that everybody learned. I remember something about a 'Cottonpicking Blues' and there were some about 'I'm going to leave you.' I think there always were songs about goodbye, I'm leaving."

mount shuffled as easily as it did L.V.: in a little spoken warm-up to "Pick Poor Robin Clean" that sounds like part of a minstrel skit, Wiley calls Thomas "Slack"—her relatives remembered that along with rolling her own Kite cigarettes, she always wore pants—and Thomas calls Wiley "Gitchee." In the East, "Geechie" would have referred to the Gullah people of Georgia and South Carolina, but in Houston, where the two women came together as a duo, "Gitchee" would have meant redhead, or country, backward, or no-'count—coming from the woman Wiley played with, it was a backhand intimacy. There is a photograph, found in a box of keepsakes that Thomas, who died in Houston in 1979, left to a niece, whose daughter shared it with Sullivan: a handsome woman posing with her feet on the running board of a 1927 Buick Roadmaster. She's hatless, with light brown skin and what might be reddish hair pulled back; she wears a light-colored dress, white stockings, and what one person looking called "serious" white pumps. A little boy in a cap peers out of the backseat. The woman might be Wiley—on the back of the picture is a name that starts with an *L*, which might be followed with an *e*—or it might be Thomas's longtime quasi-wife, or it

might be someone else.★ In 2014, when Sullivan
shared the photo with me, Wiley would have
been 106. That year our family doctor in
Berkeley mentioned that his oldest patient was a
black woman who was 106. Thomas herself,
after accepting what she called the Master and
abjuring sinful music in 1937, had spent nine
years from the late 1930s into the forties in San
Francisco, working for the Key Railroad, the
streetcar and cable car system, perhaps spending
time on Telegraph Hill at Mona's, a lesbian bar
that featured male impersonators, including such
singers as "Butch" Minton, Rose O'Neil, billed

★ "The photo will probably always remain a question
mark," Sullivan wrote me in 2015. There was writing on
the back, which at first seemed to begin with "Li." After
the *New York Times* "spent some money to get the back
restored and made legible," it looked different. Sullivan's
"best crack at the text":

> Miss Ledia Francis my
> play mother ain't she sweet
> [Third line I can't make out]
> She was just out for a
> Spin, that all.
> Now ain't she sweet.

"Play mother as I understand it." Sullivan also wrote, "was
a term that has obvious lesbian overtones among black les-
bians, but is no less often used platonically in the larger
black community."

as "Female Fred Astaire," and Gladys Bentley, "Brown Bomber of Sophisticated Songs"—why not? Why shouldn't Geeshie Wiley end up in the Bay Area herself? I couldn't help asking. "Her name is Bertha Owens," our doctor said. "Why?" I explained. "That's not her," he said. "But she did sing with Louis Armstrong."

Geeshie Wiley came out of nowhere and took a seat on a Houston train north; then she took a seat on a train back to Houston and disembarked into a nowhere just as deep. But if D. H. Lawrence was right when, in 1923, in *Studies in Classic American Literature,* speaking most specifically about Hawthorne, he wrote, "Never trust the artist. Trust the tale," the artist may not matter. Against her art, the facts of her life may be irrelevant. While the impulse to know who and why is part of being human, in the face of art other questions carry more weight. When art reaches a certain pitch, the artist disappears into her song, and we don't care who she was, where she went, what she meant. We care what the songs say.

One version of the tongue spoken over the Paramount static was, in 1930 and in many ways today, instantly recognizable, a tongue that translated itself. It's the speech of the folk-lyric song, where phrases, lines, couplets, or whole verses migrate from tune to tune, from blacks to whites and back again, without regard for subject or locale. The folk-lyric form gives you, say, the white West Virginia blues guitarist Frank Hutchison in 1926 and the black Mississippi blues guitarist Robert Johnson ten years later testifying in turn, first Hutchison, "The whole world, they sure can have my room," then Johnson, "The black man you been lovin', girlfriend, can get my room," one singer trying to say everything, the other trying to blow off the need to say anything, each according to his desire, each according to his need.

In the mouth of this tongue, every combination swallowed its origin, just as life in the United States swallowed so many blues singers, leaving them without faces or history. What emerged in the illiterate library of the folk-lyric song was stripped of any authorship. Any singer could claim words as if they were hers or his alone, stringing bits and pieces together until the common language, property of all, came forth as the testimony of a single, solitary, unique American, a speaker with as legitimate a claim on your attention as she or he could make. That's the shape "Last Kind Words Blues" takes. That's what Wiley uses to tease you, with "My mama told me," followed inevitably by "just before she died"—in the folk-lyric tradition, as opposed to the Miracles in "Shop Around," your mother never tells you *anything* until just before she dies, any more than the Mississippi River, showing up in Wiley's next verse, is ever anything but "deep and wide." But it's a setup, what one writer has called "the willful corruption of folk-lyric phrases": this is where the string is pulled. This is where the song dives into a pool of the unheard—of lines that have never been heard before, words that have never been spoken.

Wiley has already begun the song, oddly, from out of nowhere, in the middle—a beginning so strange and stark the song uses its folk-lyric chestnuts to lull you into forgetting where the song found you, and forgetting to ask where you're going to go. But before that there is a first song—a wordless, thirty-second song Wiley lines out on her guitar, a song so complete it seems wrong that any words could stand up to it.

Whoever sang lead, Thomas told McCormick of her collaborations with Wiley, played lead guitar; the other "bassed." In what Wiley plays in these wordless thirty seconds there are echoes of the chiming guitar in her fellow Texan Blind Lemon Jefferson's 1928 "See That My Grave Is Kept Clean," but they are distant echoes. What she says in her playing, which can't be separated from how she says it, to the point that any epistemological separation of form and content in Wiley's guitar passage becomes a lie, is utterly uncharacteristic of blues: a minor chord, a pulling back, a retreat, the contemplative tone of a passage that should come after the story is told, not before it.

"You know that first note of Elvie Thomas's 'Motherless Child Blues'?" the record collector Joe Bussard of Frederick, Maryland, who found the only known copy in a Baltimore junk shop in the early 1960s, said a few years ago of Thomas's playing on that song. "The first note on her guitar: *Drummmmmm* . . . That note sends me right up to the ceiling! That old Paramount sound! Sometimes I'll sit down and play that first note, five, six, eight times in a row. I'll have people over, we'll listen to that one note."

The first flat, gonging note of "Last Kind Words Blues" is almost the same—round, heavy, a stone that in an instant sinks to the bottom of a lake—but it is also muffled, then swept away, consigned to the forgotten but persisting as an echo that will infect everything that follows. For five long seconds there is a measured but propulsive momentum, steady steps forward, the need to set out, the need to arrive—and then a note lifts higher, and the player, or the mind in her fingers, is already looking back on the journey traced before. For a moment the story is stilled, and then the first pattern is repeated, but it resembles what you've heard before only as something that can be put down on paper. As language, as idea, it is something else: as one listener heard it, "not unlike a deer—being eaten alive as she looks on while her organs are pulled apart—deciding to make one last attempt to run and falling flat with a writhing motion."

With the same momentum as before, slow, measured, but the pace fraying, each note now takes a step back, not forward. The notes bear down on each other—piling up like the bodies of all those who lost themselves in the story established in the beginning of this half-minute passage, all of those we are about to meet in words.

As Wiley opens her mouth, you know that everyone in the song is already dead. "You might come here on a Sunday on a whim," the late

Richard Hugo wrote in 1973 in "Degrees of Gray in Philipsburg":

> Say your life broke down. The last good kiss
> you had was years ago. You walk these streets
> laid out by the insane, past hotels
> that didn't last, bars that did, the tortured try
> of local drivers to accelerate their lives.

Since there won't be another good kiss, there's no need to rush. "The last, kind words, I hear my daddy say," Wiley says to open the song. Blind Lemon Jefferson's "There's one kind favor, I'll ask of you" hovers over the phrase for an instant and then vanishes as Wiley stretches out *my* and *say,* diving down into the syllables as if they were pools in and of themselves, so that you understand you will never plumb their depths. *"Lawwwww-wwed,"* she says, and then, as if this is all that will ever need to be said, as if anything more would be redundant, a pointless elaboration, a decoration, kitsch, a lie, she offers nine words more:

> The last kind words, I hear my daddy say

The first four words are slightly raised, letting the next five float off elsewhere—and that is the end of the first verse of the song, all two lines of it. The verse is made to float in the sea of the song, a spar that has drifted away from whatever shipwreck it came from. It isn't the blues form, where a line is repeated, as this is, to be followed by a different, third line, a punch line. Here there is a punch, but no punch line. This is a folk-lyric fragment from long before, sometime in the 1890s, as the blues took shape, just as the opening of Elvie Thomas's "Motherless Child Blues"—

> My mama told me, just before she died
> My mama told me, just before she died
> My mama told me, just before she died
> My mama t me, just before she died
>
>   o
>
>   l
>
>   d

—with just a bare increase in pressure on the last *told,* so that it rhythmically bucks the line, gives it a slight fillip, may be the echo of an even older language. But if the words go back generations before the blues, deep into "sorrow songs," into slave songs, the feeling, the sense of the line W. C. Handy heard one day on the street and built "St. Louis Blues" around—

That man got a heart like a rock cast in the
    sea

—could not be anything but blues. It's everything the blues ever implied. It's life as the blues defined it. "The last kind words I hear my daddy say"—again, it seems complete. The song could stop right here, or repeat itself until the three minutes necessary to a commercially viable 78 rpm blues record have been registered. But the singer is going to tell you what those last kind words were—"kind" not, as Sullivan and others have written, in the sense of nice, but in a more archaic usage, meaning appropriate, proper—*He kindly passed your name on to me*—necessary, honest, even obligated, even if the words are not nice at all. "'Twas a thief said the last kind word to Christ," Robert Browning wrote. "Christ took the kindness and forgave the theft." The man in the song begins to speak.

"If I die," the man says—the singer's "daddy," in blues language her husband or her lover, but it could also be her father, because in this song nothing is stable, nothing sounds the same twice, *body* becomes *money, rich man* becomes *Richmond, sun* becomes *sign, blessèd* becomes *precious, wild*

75

becomes *wise, baby* becomes *face,* meanings fly out of the words like birds before you can name them—

> If I die, if I die
> In the German war
> *IIIIIIIIIIIIIII*

—the single word *I* stretched out across a whole line, stopping the song, a cry, a last word that can't bear to let any other follow it—

> I want you to send my body
> Send it to my mother-in-law

—which is either the all-time mother-in-law joke, pulling the rug out from under Ernie K-Doe more than thirty years in advance, or something so personal it can't quite be passed on. But whatever the man means, he can't stop. He pushes on, his words desperate, but the singer's tone accepting, knowing, calm. She heard the story before it came true. She made peace with it before she heard the news.

> 'fy get killed
> 'fy get killed

Please don't bury my soul
IIIIIIIIIIIIIII

—that *I* again, ripping a hole in the song—

I cried, just leave me out
Let the buzzards eat me whole

The words—"snippets of howls knocking around an empty landscape," as one listener described them—aren't obvious. The man could be saying he wants to be left on the battlefield, carrion and nothing more, to show that that is all war is—to show, as Yossarian would discover in the next German war when he rips open Snowden's suit and his guts spill out, that man is matter. Or he could be saying that he wants his soul to be taken into the stomach of a buzzard so it might travel the world, a spirit to bless the dead and damn the living, to bless the living and damn the dead. But as the words are not obvious, nothing about the way Wiley shapes the words is predictable.

"If I die, if I die" is modest, not desperate. It's stoic, almost comforting, not scary, leaving you defenseless, shocked, by the huge *I* that follows. The "ih" sound in the "If" is necessary to give moral weight to the aural lightness of "die" as Wiley sings the word—and to isolate the way she drops the same sound, that "ih," out of the next verse, cutting it away from the " 'fy get killed, 'fy get killed," to emphasize the harshness of the "k" sound, putting the weight of the line squarely on "killed," framing the image, the singer forcing you to see her lover's body, her husband's, her father's, as she sees it: in pieces. And yet, as Wiley sings the first "killed," she almost gives the word a curl; for an instant, it has been disarmed. Or she is about to move on.

She becomes a wanderer in her own song, and the song wanders through her. From verse to verse, it will never be clear if it is the dead man who is singing, or the woman Geeshie Wiley is playing, or her mother, or some spirit mediating between them. The first person in each successive verse has no clear owner. The drifting guitar music, punctuated by three hard, thudding notes breaking every reverie, pushes the feeling of voices calling out to each other, each shout falling just short of the ear of the person who if she heard it would be forever changed, shot forward into life, or frozen in time like Lot's wife. "People thought Dolphy avant-garde, ex-perimental," Geoff Dyer writes in *But Beautiful*, "but Mingus heard him crying out to dead slaves. Mingus had always known that that was what the blues was: music played to the dead, calling them back, showing them the way back to the living. Now he realized part of the blues was the opposite of that: the desire to be dead yourself, a way of helping the living find the dead."

The song is a séance in which the living and the dead change places until everyone is dead. Someone comes running across a field. A person arrives at a depot. A mother warns her daughter.

In 1930, the same year Geeshie Wiley recorded "Last Kind Words Blues," a guitarist named Bayless Rose recorded a tune he titled "Original Blues" for the Gennett label in Richmond, Indiana. It was a fast little jig, light, bouncy, and winking, sung in a high, raceless voice: "Mississippi, river, woman, deep and wide / Mississippi river"—the guitar sang the next phrase—"deep and wide / Can see my brown, from this other side." That was the folk-lyric artifact, passed from hand to hand and song to song for years, decades, even generations: no matter how wide the Mississippi, I can see my baby all the way across it, because I love her so much.

When Wiley comes to the lines, right after the verse in which the singer's mother speaks just before she dies, when she comes to this cut-and-dried folk pleasantry, it dissolves. She is going to empty the Mississippi into her own song. "The Mississippi river / You know it's deep and wide"—the *you know* already pressing down on the verse, raising a portent, passing a cloud over the image the words make, bringing the listener into the drama, making you watch, implicating you in the story—"I can stand right here"—

IIIIIIIIIIIIII can stand right here

—the *I can stand right here* increasing the tension, the vehemence of what's being said planting the singer on the riverbank so firmly nothing could ever blow her off her feet—

I can stand right here
See my face from the other side

She has opened the song into a realm where people turn into ghosts, ghosts turn into memories, and memories turn into curses over the fact that nothing could have turned out any differently. The singer can stand right here and see her own face from the other side. She is in two places at once. Or she is nowhere: when you see something from the other side, you see it from the vantage point of death. Unless it is always the man who died in the war who is speaking, and the singer is imagining his afterlife for him, refusing to let him go. Poe came close in "The Fall of the House of Usher," but not this close.

The words "from the other side" fade away into silence as Wiley sings them—they fade into the distance, the disappearance, that is the whole theme of the song, its words and its music, its sound and its presence. "What you do to me baby," Wiley sings to end it, sings so tenderly, her eyes sparkling for the first time in the song, "it never gets out me," and now it is clearly the woman in the song who is speaking, speaking to her dead man, ready to die herself, to traverse the oceanic metaphor that in the folk-lyric language never means anything but death:

> What you do to me baby
> It never gets out of me
> I believe I'll see you
> After I cross the deep blue sea

That's what she should say; that's what the ear translates first. That's what the song, as a product of a language shared by all, wants her to say, and it may even be what the woman in the song—not Wiley, but the fictional construct to which she's giving voice—wants to say. But Wiley takes another step back. Trust the tale, she hears a voice telling her, and then she hears the song, as the product of a single mind, a single will, singing to her, and it says what everything in the song that has come before insists that it has to say. Yes, I am ready to die. But that guarantees nothing. "What you do to me baby, it never gets out of me."

> I may not see you
> After I cross the deep blue sea

Now, there is no question that, before Sullivan's work, Geeshie Wiley's disappearance from history after 1930—and the bare traces she left before that, nothing more than a version of her nickname on a few record labels and the assumption that the sounds on the records had something to do with the name—played into the romance and the mystery of a song that is already all but in love with mystery, and *about* one's disappearance from history in ordinary life, the stories we tell about ourselves and the people we love, people we care about, people we've heard about. But this is how American folk music works. Forgetting and disappearance are the engines of its romance. They are the motor of the will in the music to create characters, to insist on their mystery and to resist the impulses of society at large to turn the music into social science—or what the late Harlem critic Albert Murray called "social science fiction."

The historical Stagger Lee, "Stag" Lee Shelton, who shot a real Billy Lyons in a real St. Louis in a real 1895, had to be forgotten before the song about him could really travel. He had to become more real as a myth than as a person, even when he was alive, even as he walked among the people who were already forgetting him, who were already singing his song. The same was true of the real people in "Frankie and Johnny," with Frankie Baker shooting Allen Britt in St. Louis in 1899, then fleeing across the country to escape the song, to escape the books written about it, the movies made from it, that had claimed all rights to her life. What about John Henry? Is it more remarkable that, sometime in the 1870s, perhaps the 1880s, perhaps in West Virginia, a railroad worker named John Henry really did die in a race with a steam drill, and then, as a real person, immediately disappeared into the legend the song made of him, and so completely that his identity has never been established—or that, as with Bob Dylan and "Ballad of Hollis Brown" or Geeshie Wiley and "Last Kind Words Blues," someone made the story up?

What did she make up? Did "Last Kind Words Blues" ultimately cause, or maybe the right word is create or mandate, the singer's disappearance? Or make it novelistically inevitable? Or lead the singer herself to become anonymous, to refuse to acknowledge her own creation, perhaps to change her name, to give up her music, to preserve her song by surrounding its mysteries with a real-life mystery, the one reinforcing and intensifying the other? That is the nation the song creates: a landscape in which an imposter, a person with a made-up name, someone who was never who she said she was, can take a stand no one else has quite taken, give a speech no one has heard before, and then vanish as if she had never been born.

In 2009, the Dex Romweber Duo—the guitarist Dex, the drummer Sara Romweber, his sister—and the guitarist Jack White tried to make a record of "Last Kind Words Blues." They did it

as a screeching, all but hysterical Broadway melo-
drama, with White making buzzard sounds until
you could feel a whole flock of them landing on
your shoulders. They ran right over the lyrics, as
if they'd never heard the record, only heard
someone talk about it. There wasn't a shred of
subtlety. It's devastating: it strips the earth.
"Whose idea was it to do that song?" I asked
White five years later. "It was God's idea," he
said. "God's."

"No, it was my idea."

In 2011, more than eighty years after Geeshie
Wiley first had her name affixed to a commercial
product, the Mekons, in 1977 a Leeds punk band
and in their present-day incarnation a Chicago-
centered group that can touch seventeenth-
century British Ranters with one hand and Patsy
Cline with another, took up the song themselves. "Jeff Tweedy"—the leader of the band
Wilco—"played me the original Wiley tune,"
Jon Langford of the Mekons said later, "and we
both scratched our heads about it." Langford
played it for Lu Edmonds, the cadaverous
Mekon who plays guitar and, it can seem, every
other stringed instrument on earth. "We set about
trying to imitate the extremely non-intuitive
structure of the song," Langford said. "It changes

where you least expect it and to our sad punk rock brains was like some weird ancient effortless math rock . . . Once we'd deciphered it enough to play it (and it actually is quite regular), Lu proceeded to chop it up into even more followable chunks." "The lyrics," he said, "were a sort of jigsaw puzzle betwixt me and Timms"—Sally Timms, the Mekons singer, at bottom an amoral country singer—"and if they are in tune with the words of the original that is further mystic magic and reptile brain thinking."

They called the song "Geeshie." It has a high-stepping "Frankie and Johnny" ragtime beat. There is piano leading, then fiddle and melodica, with Timms on all sides of the story, as if she's seen all around it, as if she's looking back. "While there's still time" is the theme of the song, and the words on their own are threatening. The way Timms sings them—"While there's / still / time"—is placid, fatalistic, unconcerned. "It is my intention to forget," she sings, looking whoever might be listening straight in the eye. "While there's still time I'll stand outside of this. While there's still time I'll resist your point of view. I'll dance around the ring while there's still time." The song goes on—but does anyone need more than this?

Others did, and others will. In 2015, Rhiannon Giddens of the Carolina Chocolate Drops, a string band remaking the music of the Negro blackface minstrel combos that flourished in parts of the country from after the Civil War into the 1930s, made "Last Kind Words Blues" the lead song on her first album under her own name. She took it as a talisman of the way that some blues can never be solved. With a smeared sound, Colin Linden's rhythm guitar sets time in motion; Giddens sings from a step behind him, and the song itself is a step behind her, as if to say there's no way to sing this song that's not too fast. Everything you say could be a lie; every hiding word in Wiley's original could be something else. Does she say "rich man" or "Richmond"? "Blessèd" or "precious"? Does Wiley promise to see her lover when she crosses the deep blue sea, or does she say that maybe she won't? Does Wiley say she'll "see my baby from the other side," or the much less earthly "see my face"? Everywhere else, Giddens makes her choices, but what she does with this last question is beyond uncanny: she sings both words at once.

In 2012, a musician and filmmaker named Kevin Barker made a Kentucky ghost-story movie called *Last Kind Words*. One day his wife read an article about the song and asked him if he knew it. "As someone seriously interested in the blues & country music of that era," he said, "that was kind of like asking me if I knew 'Stairway to Heaven.'" Geeshie Wiley sang over the closing credits. "Last kind words," Barker said, meant "kind" as "payment in kind," but he too began to float: "'Last kind words' means last earthly words before passing on to the other side." The song named Larry McMurtry's 2014 novel *Last Kind Words Saloon,* featuring Wyatt Earp and Doc Holliday wandering from Texas to Colorado to Tombstone; in its blank way the story was a match for the urban grid of the Mississippi Records album jacket. Wyatt's brother Warren is a saloon keeper; he drags his LAST KIND WORDS SALOON sign all over the West. A reporter from London, looking for the latest news on the western shootists, comes upon it: "Now the stranger was looking closely at the sign, a normal enough sign, Doc felt, though the only important word on it was 'saloon.' The rest was the sort of nonsense that interested Warren Earp." "If we come upon a saloon," Wyatt's wife, Jessie Earp, Warren's bartender, says to Warren, "what we do is: go in and make sure no kind words are spoken, and if not you'll hang up your sign." "We never did know what he meant by it," she says forty years later, when Warren is long dead and Wyatt has forgotten him. So Wiley's song migrates into other songs, songs in any form. The Mekons' "Geeshie" at least still carries her name—or, if not her real name, or the way she said and would have spelled the name she used, then her name as Paramount spelled it on the label of her records. But that won't always be so. She will go back to the nameless, the anonymous, but her presence will still be felt. As the late John Fahey, a guitarist who dedicated his life to finding the likes of Geeshie Wiley's music in his own fingers, once said, "They have no history of their own anymore, so they insinuate themselves into ours."

When people hear "Last Kind Words Blues" for the first time, they ask the same questions: What is that? Who is she? They say the same things: there is nothing like that in this world— or, as Matthew Friedberger of the Fiery Furnaces said in 2014, listening on a cell phone: "That's the most ordinary and unearthly thing I've ever heard." That voice, they say—she sounds like she's singing out of the ground, like she's been buried alive, like she doesn't mind. The truest words written about Geeshie Wiley are by the blues scholar Don Kent, in notes for an album that collected four of her and L.V. Thomas's recordings: "If Geeshie Wiley did not exist, she could not be invented." When young blues fanatics roamed the South in the 1950s and '60s, looking for rare 78s—the most prized were the most unheard, the most unknown—Wiley's name had no currency, and her song, of which only three copies have ever been found, and which not even Mack McCormick had heard when he interviewed L.V. Thomas, had been forgotten to the point of an absolute. When record collectors turned into folklorists and sought out the old singers, found Son House, Skip James, and many more, when they asked them every question under the sun, with one or two exceptions they asked nothing about a Geeshie Wiley, because aside from a single track on an early-'60s reissue album they'd never heard anything, not a name, not a song, to make them ask. Her songs did not really begin to travel until 1994, by way of Terry Zwigoff's movie *Crumb*, about the cartoonist and onetime record collector R. Crumb. He walks through his own story as a sour, bitter, misanthropic nihilist, until he stops in front of a shelf of 78s. He pulls out a record, puts it on a turntable, and lies down on a bed. As the first notes of Geeshie Wiley's song appear on the soundtrack he begins to talk about "the common people," about "their way of expressing a connection to eternity, or whatever you want to call it"—embarrassed by the way the pathos of his words has cut them loose from his folk-music ideology, at how he has shown his true feelings, he tries to dismiss his own words, to bury the fact that, as he listened, the music took him out of himself. He tries to push himself back into the shell of someone who hates everything, but for a moment he can't. At that moment, in 1994, Wiley might have been present to say what she thought, but no one knew where to look. Aside from Mack McCormick and his transcript filed away more than thirty years before, no one knew her real name. And if she was alive, she wasn't talking. Certain crucial facts have now been established, but the records still call out to the woman behind them, trying to pull her out from behind the curtain of their static, so we are free to tell any story we like.

She was born in Oklahoma. As a girl with reddish hair, other children called her "Geech"—a slur for Cherokee. Maybe they were right: there had been a lot of free blacks on the Trail of Tears.

She softened the name, but she liked it—Lillie Mae was so common.

Not two years after she and L.V. Thomas recorded in Wisconsin, the Depression forced Paramount into bankruptcy. There were no more records. She and Thomas performed on the street, and began an affair. When her husband found out he came at her with his hands; she pulled a knife and killed him, stabbing down into his neck. She spent six months in jail before her case came to trial; the judge threw it out. In 1933 she and L.V. traveled through Virginia and North Carolina as part of a Negro blackface minstrel troupe, the Aloysius Persons Ethiopian Head-Spinners, playing Tambo and Bones to the delight of all-black audiences. Then L.V. went back to Houston. When they split up, L.V. took a picture of Wiley standing on a friend's car: "Hike your leg up like Bonnie Parker!" L.V. shouted.

Soon Wiley was cleaning houses in Memphis. She lived off men. Her life slowed. She played out when she could; one night she sang "Pick Poor Robin Clean" at a juke joint in Clarksdale, watching a white woman in the crowd with a camera. She didn't see her shooting her as she went onto the floor to dance, but when her

picture appeared in *Life* magazine, part of a series of FSA photographs of the South, she was
pleased that Marion Post Wolcott had showed her
only from behind.

One of her men turned her out. "I'm a hus-
tling coon, that's just what I am," she'd sung in
"Pick Poor Robin Clean," at once defiant and
resigned, so *So what of it?* "I'm gonna cut your
throat, baby, I'll look down in your face," she
sang sweetly in her "Skinny Leg Blues," but she
didn't, and not because she already had. She'd
seen the faces of other women her pimp had cut.
So she ran. On the outskirts of town, approaching
a clearing lit with gas lanterns, she found herself
drawn into a revival. She didn't know why; she

wasn't a believer. On the edges of the crowd, standing apart, she saw a group of about twenty men and women, mostly white but a few of them black, the men in old-fashioned suits and boots, the women in long white dresses. They were the Lamb Family, they said, singers and seekers after what they called New Harmony. At the center was Zandervon Orbeliah Lam, a big man with a huge white moustache: the Shepherd. As the revival preacher railed down his stentorian, up-and-down cadences—

And what the LORD wants
The LORD gets
What YOU want
The LORD hates

—the family walked off slowly, Wiley among them, singing "If Tonight Should End the World" and "See That My Grave Is Kept Green" under their breath.

Like the Shakers, who believed that Jesus was not a prophet but an avatar, a first coming of which they were the second, the devotees of New Harmony believed that to touch the truth one had to lose oneself in song, but the song had to be of this earth. Traveling out of the South, toward Portland, Oregon, where they had heard God appeared in the rain to cleanse his children, Wiley sang "Careless Love," "Little Brown Dog," "Nottamun Town." But in Portland, with its open parks, the welcoming streets, the lack of fear in the air, New Harmony had barely found a house before the followers began to leave it. When the Shepherd disappeared with three of his nearly grown daughters by two of his wives, Wiley like the rest found herself on the street.

She heard that Frankie Baker, the real Frankie of all the Frankie and Johnny songs, lived in Portland; she wasn't hard to find. She'd come there years before, because she loved roses, and to get away from the song, from people pointing at her on the streets, singing the song at her, the verses about how she slept with the judge who acquitted her. But the song had arrived in Portland long before she did; her house was a tourist attraction. Wiley knocked on the door; she told Baker she had a song to sing her. Once inside, she began to sing "Frankie." *No, no, not that, get out, you get out now,* Baker shouted at her. No, Wiley said, you haven't heard it like this. This won't make you ashamed.

She sang the tune slowly, flattening the sing-songy choruses and the fox-trot rhythm that the number had taken on over the decades with a hint of the ragtime Baker knew from St. Louis in 1899, when Frankie shot her pimp, who had beaten her for coming home short. Now Wiley made the sound of a life being dragged across time, and for a moment all the guilt and rage and pride that had haunted Baker for more than forty years fell away. After that, Wiley lived with Baker and ran her shoeshine stand. She took the house as her own in the early 1950s, when Baker went mad and was sent to the state hospital. She began to go by Lillian. Geeshie sounded strange in the Northwest, and Lillie Mae was too country.

One day in 1957, in Seattle, where she was visiting friends, she read that Elvis Presley was coming to town. She'd heard his "Hound Dog" on the radio. She was curious who this person might be—a white boy singing those old hound dog songs of her childhood—so she talked her way into Sick's Seattle Stadium. "I used to clean house for Mrs. Presley in Memphis," she told a guard. "She called me and asked me to tell her how her boy did." Inside, she sat down next to a teenager; there weren't many other black people there. "Why are you here?" she asked him. "James Marshall Hendricks, ma'am," the boy who in ten years would be known as Jimi Hendrix said to her; he'd been raised to speak politely, especially to older people. "I'm here to see the king." After what seemed like hours of the kind of vaudeville show Wiley had hated even as a girl—an acrobat, a juggler, a tap dancer, a comedian—the person they had come to see took the stage. "I always like to begin my concerts with the National Anthem," he said. "Would you all please rise?" They rose. Elvis twisted his body into a Z and grabbed the microphone stand as if it were a flagpole. "YOU AIN'T NOTHIN' BUT A HOUND DOG" were the only words anyone could really hear as the whole house exploded with pleasure: in that moment, it was their national anthem. Wiley and the boy hugged each other, jumping up and down. Later, he visited her in Portland. She taught him chords he had never been able to find.

In the 1960s, in the New Harmony dress she always kept perfect, she'd play for tips in the Park Blocks, near the Lincoln statue. She liked how unheroic he looked, how ordinary—how needy. Almost every day, she'd play "I Am a Man of Constant Sorrow," a song she'd first heard in the 1920s—people knew it now, because it was on the first album by a folk singer named Bob Dylan. He sang it loudly, as if he was sure you didn't believe him; that wasn't her style. The first man to record the song, Emry Arthur, could hardly do more than bang the guitar. He'd been shot through the hands; as Dock Boggs, one of the men who played with him once put it, "He couldn't reach the chords."

Wiley could. She could charm them as if they were snakes. She'd been captivated by Arthur's record, which she'd bought herself, even though she couldn't afford the kind of big, varnished players the company she'd end up recording for made. She loved the swaying rhythm, the "Say goodbye to old Kentucky"—the "say goodbye" to anywhere—and especially the end, when the singer imagines other people he knows, people he doesn't, the whole human race, going on with their lives of love and money "while I am sleeping in the clay," the singer dreaming of a life they will never live, even in death. She imagined herself dead, the red earth all around her, the earth itself her shroud, and it was there, in that waking dream, on the train to Wisconsin, that she wrote "Last Kind Words Blues."

Some of the words were old, passed down, inevitable, words from a thousand other songs that she shifted just barely, as if listening to the wind between them. Some came to her from places she couldn't name—snatches of conversation she'd overheard in a bar, maybe, a random, broken sentence that had formed in her mind years before but had never come out of her mouth. Some of the words as they attached themselves to each other made no sense to her at all, nothing she would have explained if she could, but they felt as true as they were out of reach.

She wrote carefully, letting the notes on the guitar lead the words, slowly, as always, until she had it right. Until the song had so shaped itself it felt like she hadn't written it at all—it felt like someone else had written it, and it was her privilege to hear it, and pass it on. To live it out, as she sang, even all those years later. To enact it, as small groups of people, black and white, old and young, gathered around her in the park, while others merely paused for a moment on their way to somewhere else.

NOTES

Last Kind Words 1926–1953 (Mississippi, 2006). Cover paintings by Chris Johanson. Lettering by Johanna Jackson.

There are many CD collections and publications chronicling the story of Paramount Records. The extraordinarily elaborate box sets *The Rise and Fall of Paramount Records, Volume 1* (Third Man/Revenant, 2013) and *The Rise and Fall of Paramount Records 1928–1932* (2014)—comprising LPs, artifacts, reproductions of advertisements, artist biographies, detailed and imaginative historical chronicles, and thumb drives together containing 1600 recordings—constitute the ruling historical record. See also Alex van der Tuuk, *Paramount's Rise and Fall: The Roots and History of Paramount Records* (Denver: Mainspring Press, 2012), and Amanda Petrusich, *Do Not Sell at Any Price: The Wild, Obsessive Hunt for the World's Rarest 78 rpm Records* (New York: Scribner, 2014).

Geeshie Wiley, "Last Kind Words Blues," "Skinny Leg Blues" (released 1930), "Pick Poor Robin Clean," and "Eagles on a Half" (released 1931), Elvie Thomas, "Motherless Child Blues," and Wiley and Thomas, "Over to My House" (released 1930) are included on *The Rise and Fall of Paramount Records, 1928–1932* and on *Mississippi Blues—Vol. 1 (1928–1937)* (Document, 1993), and best heard on the currently out of print *American Primitive Vol. II—Pre-War Revenants (1897–1939)* (Revenant, 2005), a collection of recordings by performers about whom, when the set appeared, almost nothing was known, including Bayless Rose, the Nugrape Twins, Homer Quincy Smith (the soul-shaking "I Want Jesus to Talk with Me"), Two Poor Boys, and the deeper than deep Mattie May Thomas. See John Jeremiah Sullivan's piece on the compilation, "Unknown Bards," collected in his *Pulphead* (New York: Farrar, Straus and Giroux, 2011).

"Bed of static." "Vol. 30: Last Kind Words Blues," *Perfect Pop Singles* (blog), October 9, 2011, perfectpopsingles.wordpress.com/2011/10/09.

John Jeremiah Sullivan, "The Ballad of Geeshie and Elvie," *New York Times Magazine,* April 13, 2014. The online edition includes links to all Wiley/Thomas recordings; much embedded video, by Leslye Davis, of interviews with Mack Mc-Cormick, L.V. Thomas's relatives and parishioners; illustrations not included in the print edition; and a 2014 recording of "Last Kind Words Blues" by the Kronos Quartet. I also had the benefit of Sullivan's much longer essay "Next Kind Words: On the Trail of a Few American Phantoms," as of this writing unpublished.

Sister Idell Murray, "Sister L.V.'s voice." Courtesy John Jeremiah Sullivan.

L.V. Thomas, "There were blues," and following. Sullivan, "The Ballad of Geeshie and Elvie."

Frank Hutchison, "Worried Blues" (Okeh, 1926), on Hutchison, *Complete Recorded Works in Chronological Order, Volume 1, 1926–1929* (Document, 1997).

Robert Johnson, "I Believe I'll Dust My Broom" (Vocalion, 1936), on Johnson, *The Centennial Collection—The Complete Recordings* (Columbia Legacy, 2011).

Joe Bussard, "You know that first note." Conversation with GM, 1999.

"Not unlike a deer." Andreea Scarlat, "Last Words." New School University, New York, 2014.

Richard Hugo, "Degrees of Gray in Philipsburg" (collected in *The Lady in Kicking Horse Reservoir,* 1973), from *Making Certain It Goes On: The Collected Poems of Richard Hugo* (New York: Norton, 1984).

Robert Browning, *The Ring and the Book* (1868–1869).

"Snippets of howls." Jean Garnett, "Music Wars." New School University, New York, 2012.

Geoff Dyer, *But Beautiful: A Book about Jazz* (New York: North Point, 1996), 199–20.

Bayless Rose, "Original Blues," collected on *American Primitive Vol. II—Pre-War Revenants*.

Dex Romweber Duo featuring Jack White, "Last Kind Words Blues" (Third Man, 2009).

Jon Langford on "Geeshie." E-mail to GM, August 12, 2013.

Mekons, "Geeshie," *Ancient & Modern 1911–2011* (Bloodshot/ Sin, 2011). The lyrics continued: "Nothing happens twice. Raise a glass of wine and try to still time. Gonna build this empty space while there's still time. Gonna drag my cart piled high while there's still time. Gonna build another bomb and hope the doctor comes while there's still time. Trail across the map, they'll be dragging something back across the ashes and the stones. Save the bones from Henry Jones, while there's still time. To the splendor and the crimes. Nothing happens twice. Raise a glass of wine and try to still time."

Larry McMurtry, *The Last Kind Words Saloon* (New York: Liverwright, 2014).

John Fahey quoted by Scott Blackwood, "Out of Their Anonymous Dark," notes to *American Primitive Vol. II: Pre-War Revenants*.

Rhiannon Giddens, "Last Kind Words," *Tomorrow Is My Turn* (Nonesuch, 2015).

Last Kind Words. Written and directed by Kevin Barker (RLJ, 2012). Barker, "As someone," from promotional material.

John Fahey, "They have no history." Quoted in Scott Blackwood, "Out of Their Anonymous Dark," liner notes to *American Primitive Vol. II—Pre-War Revenants*.

Matthew Friedberger, "That's the most." Conversation with GM, 2014.

Don Kent, notes to *Mississippi Masters: Early American Blues Classics* (Yazoo, 1994).

Crumb, directed by Terry Zwigoff (Sony Pictures Classics, 1994).

Everything in the last section of this chapter is made up, but some of the characters are real, albeit in mostly fictional roles. Zandervon Orbeliah Lam of Virginia did lead a singing group called the Lamb Family; as Bela Lam and His Greene County Singers they recorded "See That My Grave Is Kept Green" in 1927 (see *Rural String Bands of Virginia,* County, 1993) and "If Tonight Should End the World" in 1929 (see the anthology *Virginia Roots: The 1929 Richmond Sessions,* Outhouse, 2002). Frankie Baker did move to Portland; she died in the state mental hospital in 1952. Elvis Presley played Sick's Seattle Stadium on September 1, 1957, and began his show with "Hound Dog" as the National Anthem; a fourteen-year-old Jimi Hendrix was there. Bob Dylan recorded "Man of Constant Sorrow" for his first album—good, but not as good as his race against Blind Lemon Jefferson's "See That My Grave Is Kept Clean." Emry Arthur's 1928 version, the first recording of the song—which Arthur, born around 1900 in backwoods Tennessee, may have learned from his sometime musical partner Dick Burnett, a blind minstrel who some claim composed the song in 1912—can be heard on Arthur's *I Am a Man of Constant Sorrow Volume One* (Old Homestead, 2001), though perhaps better on the anthology *The Music of Kentucky: Early American Rural Classics 1927–37, Vol. 2* (Yazoo, 1995).

The photo of a woman posing on a 1927 Buick Roadmaster is from a box of keepsakes that L.V. Thomas left to her niece Dally May, who passed it to her daughter Paula Ransom, who provided it to John Jeremiah Sullivan and Leslye Davis, who in turn provided it to me. It is used here by the kind permission of Paula Ransom. All rights reserved. It may not be used in any other manner in any other medium. Sullivan's researcher Joel Finsel adds this detail regarding the likely date and scene of the photograph, based on its striking borders: "My mother, Rebecca Finsel, who trades in antiquities, found some photographs with identical borders somebody took of a fishing trip. She pointed out that the tiny symbols in the border around the photo are miniature artist palettes with tiny paint brushes and easels with blank canvases on each. The similarly bordered antique photos she found on eBay both hailed from Crockett, Texas, c. 1920–30s. When we contacted the seller of these photos on eBay, they mentioned that borders such as these were often unique to the processing labs. Crockett Lake is about 2 hours north of Houston."

The photo of a woman dancing is Marion Post Wolcott, *Negroes Jitterbugging in a juke joint on Saturday afternoon. Clarksdale, Mississippi Delta,* November 1939, a Farm Security Administration work now in the Library of Congress.

World Upside Down
"I Wish I Was a Mole in the Ground,"
Bascom Lamar Lunsford

"A folk song has a thousand faces and you must meet them all if you want to play this stuff," Bob Dylan wrote in 2004. "A folk song might vary in meaning and it might not appear the same from one moment to the next. It depends on who's playing and who's listening."

Bascom Lamar Lunsford's "I Wish I Was a Mole in the Ground" is a song with a thousand faces. It's an old American folk song—no one knows how old.

It's 1928. Lunsford, a lawyer and song-catcher from Madison County, North Carolina, puts the song across in a flat, plaintive, aching tone that scrambles time. From one moment to the next he might be contemplating something altogether imprisoned in the past, an instant of fright, a face so blurred by time he has to reinvent its features. He'll tip over into a metaphysical half-light where words must be dragged from the throat and pushed into the light, where human beings turn into animals and back again. He'll jump into a different day, a different lifetime, and pull himself and whoever might be listening directly into the present, where all choices are open, nothing has been settled, and danger is so close you can smell it, then hoist his voice up as if he's pulling up his trousers to deliver a political speech at a county fair where no one is listening, then start all over again, retracing a circle, with the shadings of his singing making all signposts appear just slightly out of place. His voice grows in presence from verse to verse, until, in the face of the world it is describing, it feels omnipresent, as if the singer has seen all around the world.

Lunsford plays the banjo, but the banjo seems to be tracing some different song. The notes are bright, bouncing, quickstepping through his fingers like grasshoppers. But in the sameness of the patterns they trace, the notes subtly quieting as the next verse looms up, making a kind of negative fanfare, you feel an undertow, an inexorable rhythm pulling you into an impenetrable fatalism, where what you want, what you wish for, is of no account to time, nature, the men and

women before you, the girls and boys who will
follow you, as you write your name on water,
"and the great shroud of the sea rolled on as it
rolled five thousand years ago." You can feel the
quiet, comforting, drowning swell and ebb of
the waves, and slip right down, smiling over that
bouncy, circular pattern on the banjo, the sense
that life is a joke, that it will never change, that
it will always trip you up. Bascom Lamar Lunsford walks into a bar and he never knows what
the bartender is going to say to him. "I'll have
my regular, Pete." "Who are you? And what's
that moleskin doing on your head?"

This is the story the song tells in words, as
Lunsford sang them in 1928, in a recording
studio in Ashland, Kentucky:

> I—
> Wish I was a mole in the ground
> Yes I wish I was a mole in the ground
> Like a—
> Mole in the ground
> I'd root that mountain down and I
> Wish I was a mole in the ground
>
> Oh Tempe wants a nine-dollar shawl
> Yes Tempe wants a nine-dollar shawl

When I come o'er the hill with a forty-dollar
    bill 'tis
Hmm baby where you been so long

I—been in the Bend so long
Yes I been in the Bend so long
I been in the Bend with the rough and rowdy
    men 'tis
Baby where you been so long

Oh I don't like
A railroad man
No I don't like
A railroad man
If I'se a railroad man they'll
Kill you when he can
And drink up your blood like wine

Oh I wish I was a lizard in the spring
Yes I wish I was a lizard in the spring
Like a—lizard in the spring I'd hear my darlin'
    sing and I
Wish I was a lizard in the spring

Oh Tempe
Let your hair
Roll down
Tempe
Let your hair roll down

Let your hair roll down and your bangs curl
   around oh
Tempe let your hair roll down

I wish I was a mole in the ground
Yes I wish I was a—
Mole in the ground
Like a mole in the ground I'd root that moun-
   tain down and I
Wish I was a mole in the ground

Lunsford, born in 1882 in Madison County, North Carolina, was forty-six. He was recording for the Brunswick label of New York City, making a commercial recording he hoped would be a hit. It was the same year he founded the Mountain Dance and Folk Festival in Asheville, North Carolina—where he last appeared in 1973, at the age of ninety-one, just a month before he died. If he'd lived a hundred more years than he did, he might not have been able to assume all the faces the song contained.

It's a song that calls for great deeds, for the overturning of the world itself. As the unnatural flips to the pastoral and back again, the song wraps itself in its own mystery, its own darkness and blinding light, in the degraded, puny, repulsive, frightening image of its own name, proclaiming the wish of a man to be a mole—a mystery that today, singing the song in studios or onstage, or listening in their own rooms, people are still trying to solve.

"Listen to 'I Wish I Was a Mole in the Ground' again and again," the historian Robert Cantwell wrote in 1991, in an essay later adapted for *When We Were Good,* Cantwell's book on the 1960s folk revival, a movement in which Bascom Lamar Lunsford was a living icon—or, as John Cohen of the New Lost City Ramblers once put it, a "mystical god." "Learn to play the banjo and sing it yourself over and over again," Cantwell said, "study every printed version, give up your career and maybe your family, and you will not fathom it."

It's a folk-lyric song—a song that came together over unknowable years out of bits and pieces of older songs, jokes, slang phrases, curses, until it gained a kind of shape that would in some way hold it together, that would allow it to carry its title longer than anyone could carry its tune. It is an authorless folk song that makes authors out of listeners. As with Walter Benjamin in 1934, in "The Author as Producer":

An author who teaches a writer nothing teaches nobody anything. The determining factor is the exemplary character of a production that enables it, first, to lead other producers to this production, and secondly to present them with an improved apparatus for their use. And this apparatus is better to the degree that it leads consumers to production, in short that it is capable of making co-workers out of readers or spectators.

That's what the song does. Dropped down into a surrealist parlor game, people hear the song and make up their own versions, just like that. Give someone "I wish I was" and an ocean rolls out. The song rewrites itself:

> I wish I was a bird in a tree
> I wish I was a bird in a tree
> If I was a bird in a tree I'd never want to flee
> And I wish I was a bird in a tree
>
> I wish I was a killer in the sand
> I wish I was a killer in the sand
> If I was a killer in the sand I'd set fire to the land
> And I wish I was a killer in the sand
>
> I wish I was a dream in the night
> I wish I was a dream in the night

> If I was a dream in the night I'd give you second
>   sight
> And I wish I was a dream in the night

Even Lunsford himself could never stop. The version he sang almost never varied, but he collected many more:

> I wish I was a mole in the ground
> Oh I wish I was a mole in the ground
> I'd turn this wide world around
>
> Oh I wish I was a lizard in the spring
> Oh I wish I was I lizard in the spring
> I would kiss old Lizer Jane
> Oh I am as free as a little bird can be

The song is not only unfathomable, it's irresistible, and what's irresistible about it is altogether rooted in its unfathomableness. In 1966, thirty-eight years after Lunsford recorded in 1928—and fourteen years after Harry Smith made it one of the eighty-four records he brought together to make his *Anthology of American Folk Music,* in 1952—Bob Dylan found himself tangled in the song. It got under his skin; it came out in "Memphis Blues Again." Against a light, then surging background, with the organ flowing easily, then ignoring the rhythm of the band to find its own frantic pileup of high notes, Dylan sang with bitter wonder:

> Mona tried to tell me
> To stay away from the train line
> She said that all the railroad men
> Just drink up your blood like wine
> And I said Oh I didn't know that
> But then again there's only one I've met
> And he just smoked my eyelids
> And punched my cigarette

There's a translation of Lunsford's lines as filtered through Dylan's in a drawing by an artist named Sofia Falcone: an old photo of railroad men, gathered on the tracks, dressed from somewhere between the 1890s and the 1920s, coats and ties, collarless shirts, one man in overalls, another in a college cardigan, with red stains on their hands and clothes, with one man, half hidden behind another, holding a wine glass almost full to the brim below his waist, as if to hide it. Are they railroad workers, drunk every Saturday, leaving someone dead on a barroom floor at the end of the night? Or the owners, bleeding every worker down to his toes? In this picture you can't tell, any more than you can finger the railroad men in Dylan's song or Lunsford's. You make your own answer as you translate the image for your own purposes, or you give yourself up to the fact that you will never know. As Dylan defined folk music in 1965:

All the authorities who write about what it is and what it should be, when they say keep it simple, that it should be easily understood—folk music is the only music where it isn't simple. It's never been simple. It's weird . . . I've never written anything hard to understand, not in my head anyway, and nothing so far out as some of the old songs . . . "Little Brown Dog." "I bought a little brown dog, its face is all gray. Now I'm going to Turkey flying on my bottle." And "Nottamun Town," that's like a herd of ghosts passing through on the way to Tangiers.

If "I Wish I Was a Mole in the Ground," as Lunsford recorded it in 1928, is alluring and obscure in its words and its cadence—that banjo rolling over hills and valleys, the feeling that Lunsford began playing long before the engineer started recording and kept playing long after the record was made, the odd disassociation of the singing and the playing, as if the banjo is playing itself, that this is all part of some greater song, its beginning and the end dropping over opposite horizons as the song turns you in one direction and another—the song is clear and direct as a product of technology. Made just after electrical recording with microphones replaced the system where the musician had to sing and play into a conical horn, the performance carries the modern world with it. The performer is almost physically present. But earlier recordings of the song carry the sense of something far away, something already receding into the past, something hard to speak of, something it might be forbidden to think of. Lunsford always said he learned the song from a classmate of his from Rutherford College, Fred Moody, in 1901, as they were waiting for a train back to their home counties in the mountains outside of Asheville. And it was Moody, of Jonathan's Creek, Haywood County, who made the first recording of "I Wish I Was a Mole in the Ground," in 1921, in Buncombe County, North Carolina, where the folklorist Frank C. Brown of Duke University had gone to find singers who knew old songs. He recorded them on one-minute cylinders; today you can hear the needle in the deep grooves before you can hear anything else. Even so, you can think the distortion off—and there, with the first verse and the two Tempe verses, Moody's high, curling tone is like its own scratch. His voice wraps around itself like a snake. He sounds more like a ghost than a man. In his brief moment in history, it's as if he's merely passing by, he and a couple of other farmers on their way to a dance. It's not artless. Moody has met those thousand faces; he looks them in the eye.

Not three years later, in 1924, Lunsford, whom Brown also recorded, though not with this song, is trying to make the first commercial recording of "I Wish I Was a Mole in the Ground," for the Okeh label, in Atlanta, singing into that pre-electric horn—and he's not ready. He's hesitant, unsure, clumsy, stepping back from those faces staring out at him. The song wants something from whoever presumes to play it— something Lunsford, perhaps afraid of the machine, perhaps afraid of the song, afraid of failing the song, or afraid of the person he has to become to sing the song, isn't ready to give. The record is a fumbling blur. There's no emotion, no promise, no threat. The huge, magisterial voice of 1928 isn't even a fantasy.

Today teenagers in Charlottesville, Virginia, sing the song on spirit walks through graveyards. They're not afraid to sing the song to the dead, or in a deeper sense, maybe closer to the heart of the song, to let the dead sing the song to them. Though in 1902, just before she died, Lunsford's mother asked him to sing her "I Wish I Was a Mole in the Ground"—"It was the last request she ever made of me," he said in 1949—in 1924 he couldn't do it. He turned and went back to his everyday life.

He started out in the beginning of the twentieth century traveling the mountains selling seedlings. He taught high school and college. He earned a law degree from Trinity College, which became Duke University. He worked as a beekeeper, practiced law, served as a judge, ran a newspaper, managed political campaigns—the B-side of one of his 78s, recorded for Columbia in 1930, was "A Stump Speech in the Tenth District" (the A-side was "Speaking the Truth"). During the First World War he went to work for the Justice Department tracking down draft dodgers in New York City. He worked for the North Carolina legislature and the New Deal—and at any time, as a friend of his once put it, he'd "cross hell on a rotten bridge" to find a song he hadn't heard, one of those thousand faces he never stopped counting. As he put it in 1935, while recording his "Memory Collection" of ballads and other songs for an archive at Columbia University—he used the mountain word *ballets*—he'd taken on the work of preserving the legacy of the Appalachians because "I'm one of them myself." As the "Minstrel of the Appalachians," he was putting the music into the record "in the spirit of the one who said, 'I shot an arrow, in the air / It fell to earth, I know not where / But long years after, still unbroke / I found that arrow, in the heart of an oak.'" He paused for a half second, and then went on, with passion now, with a lift in his voice, speaking slightly less slowly: "'I breathed a song into the air / It came to earth I know not where / But long years after, from beginning to end'"—and here he slows the pace again, not letting the punch line out until even the imaginary audience of this day is leaning toward him—"'I found that song in the heart of a friend.'"

Twenty and twenty-five years later, in the late 1950s and early 1960s, in Greenwich Village, Philadelphia, Minneapolis, Berkeley, people began to sing "I Wish I Was a Mole in the Ground" again, looking for something in the song they couldn't find anywhere else. Certainly not on the radio. In *Chronicles,* Bob Dylan wrote about pop music in the early 1960s—about Ricky Nelson, about how much he liked him, about an affinity he sensed between Ricky Nelson and himself. But no matter how good the likes of "Travelin' Man" might be, he said, "It was all a mistake." It had no future, because the future was in the past, in those old songs where nothing was simple. "What was not a mistake," Dylan said, "was the ghost of Billy Lyons, rootin' the mountain down, standing 'round East Cairo, Black Betty bam be lam. That was no mistake. That's the stuff that was happening. That's the stuff that could make you question what you'd always accepted." That's the crux: a song, a way of singing a song, that could call anything into question. And if that's what you were looking for—and the impulse of that moment in history, 1959, 1960, 1961, 1962, was, in that direction, gaining the momentum of a runaway train—what in the world could even come close to a song that was also a mystical incantation, a metaphysical romance, a Grimm's fairy tale, a horror story, a tune Lunsford often described as "a typical song" of his Pigeon River Valley, which makes you wonder what kind of haunted house the Pigeon River Valley could be? What could come close to something that begins, "I wish I was a mole in the ground"?

> I wish I was a mole in the ground
> I wish I was a mole in the ground
> Like a mole in the ground
> I'd root that mountain down
> And I wish I was a mole in the ground

You can see someone standing on a hilltop, "looking down," as a floating blues lyric puts it, "on the house where I used to live," or that same person walking the streets of what Robert Johnson called a "strange man's town," a place where every face is a mask and everyone expects to see right through you, that person imagining, conjuring up a mountain only to bring it down, that he or she is the president, Jesus Christ, or the Antichrist. It could be Bascom Lamar Lunsford, in 1928, singing a song that could not be typical of anything, or Marianne Faithfull, as she recorded the song eighty years later.

Whoever it is, if the moment is right the singer sings the song, and the song sings the singer. The song is so extreme in its demands that it becomes almost abstract—and in its abstraction, if the singer can give himself or herself over to the song, neither the singer nor the song can lie. "Well, I wished I was a mole in the ground / I wished I was a mole in the ground / I was a mole in the ground, and I'd tear, I'd tear, I'd tear this mountain down / Wished I was a mole in the ground," as Faithfull sang it in 2009, perhaps more than anyone before her sounding like she'd already done it. Changing yourself into vermin, a pest—it's a comforting thought. It's more than that. It's satisfying. It's thrilling. You are burrowing under the mountain, under the world, until it all comes crashing down. Or until a picture of that Judgment Day presents itself: once, Lunsford wrote in 1934, around Vashti, in Alexander County in North Carolina, "the people of the countryside were filled with superstitious consternation, when during a terrible storm, about an acre of earth and rock on Sugarloaf Mountain sank some several feet. Some thought it an ill omen, while others sang: 'If I was a mole in the ground / I'd root old Sugarloaf down.'"

Who could resist? The song from its first note is political to the point of nihilism. It asks people to say what they want, what they wish for, who they would like to be, the way they want the world to be—or if they want the world to be at all. "I wish I was—" The song immediately demands that you account for yourself: a fundamental democratic act. It demands that you speak the truth, that you dredge up your most forbidden and unholy thoughts, that you rewrite the song in your own words.

But if "I Wish I Was a Mole in the Ground" is irreducibly political, it is also absolutely carnal—from the nine-dollar shawl Tempe wants to what she'll give you when she gets it. Bob Neuwirth is a painter and a singer who was Bob Dylan's sidekick in the mid-sixties—you can see him in the film *Don't Look Back,* reminding Dylan of the "rolling stone" verse when Dylan and Joan Baez are trying to sing Hank Williams's "Lost Highway." From then to now, Neuwirth has always gone for the sexual heart of the song—and all he had to do to open up the tune, to translate it, to take it out of its riddles and make its metaphors into plain speech, was change one word, as he performed the song in 1999, playing with the British fiddler and singer Eliza Carthy. It's all in the way Neuwirth, then only days from sixty, turns to Carthy, twenty-three, and the look on his face as he sings: "I wish I was a lizard in your spring." Carnal, lascivious, the dirty old man in the flower garden, but at the end Neuwirth too wants the whole world, turning once more to Carthy: "I wish we were all moles in the ground." He could be echoing Camus in *The Rebel:* "Because I rebel, we exist."

With teenagers singing the song in grave-yards, with Bob Neuwirth using the song as a seduction right onstage, from anbb (the composer Alva Noto and the singer Blixa Bargeld of Einstürzende Neubauten) in a robotic-techno hysterical-industrial rendition in 2010 (at the end, as in the 1956 sci-fi horror movie *The Mole People,* the moles really do come out of the ground) to a farmer's market singer in Berkeley whose face looks as if it was carved up by a knife and healed in the woods, to a betrayed husband, an abandoned wife, a hermit who hasn't had sex in thirty years and never thinks of anything else singing new verses to the song to themselves, to, you can imagine, crowds singing "Like a mole in the ground I will root that mountain down" in Tahrir Square in Cairo, in Taksim Gezi Park in Istanbul, at anti-austerity marches in Athens and Lisbon, at Umbrella demonstrations in Hong Kong, at Tea Party rallies on the National Mall, outside the statehouse in Madison, Wisconsin, or from the balconies of the Senate chambers in

Austin, Texas, we are already a long way from Bascom Lamar Lunsford's original, but the point is there is no original.

No one knows how the song came together. As Robert Cantwell sums it up, "The lizard and the mole, Tempe's curls and her nine-dollar shawl, rough convicts and long days behind bars,★ the treacherous railroad men—what unseen incidents tie these images together we can only guess." All of the lines in the song, every picture, every word, migrated into this song from other songs. Each of the lines in Lunsford's song is an orphan seeking brothers and sisters, and finding them, making a new family, then sending their progeny into the world to find their own way.

The song presents an indelible, seductive image of what in seventeenth-century England, when the king had been deposed and executed and Ranters and Levellers were acting as if all truths were lies, was called "a world upside

---

★ In some songs dating to the nineteenth or early twentieth century, "the Bend" referred to the Tennessee State Penitentiary, and in "I Wish I Was a Mole in the Ground" singers often changed "the bend" to "the pen." Lunsford always insisted that it was a reference not to any prison but to "the bend in the Pigeon River"—"known," he allowed in 1949, "for outbreaks of crime, occasionally."

down"—a time when a mole could root down a mountain. The phrase became a song: "World Upside Down," according to some sources a broadside published in 1643, when King Charles I was caught in the English Civil War. It was sung at Yorktown in 1781, near the end of the American Revolution, though historians and folklorists disagree if it was victorious Continental Army troops who were singing it, or their British captives.★ For despite Bob Neuwirth's untangling of the lizard in the spring, the song remains full of black holes, blank spots. And one of those black holes in the song is an image that in its way is as strange as any mole or lizard or blood-drinking railroad man: the forty-dollar bill.

In 2015 a freelance writer and part-time lecturer at the Community College of Philadelphia, Sindhu Zagoren was a banjo player and a graduate student at the University of North Carolina in Chapel Hill when in 2004 she sang "Mole in the

★ As the version from *The Burl Ives Songbook* runs: "If buttercups buzz'd after the bee / If boats were on land, churches on sea / If ponies rode men and if grass ate the cows / And cats should be chased into holes by the mouse / If the mamas sold their babies / To the gypsies for half a crown / If summer were spring and the other way round / Then all the world would be upside down."

Ground" on DJ Rupture's album *Special Gun-powder*. She first heard the song in Boston, where she's from: "I experimented with the song for some years," she says, "eventually shifting to a minor key, which I thought went well with the eerie lyrics." She met DJ Rupture—also known as Jace Clayton—in Barcelona, where they recorded the song in his home studio.

Wish I was a mole in the ground
Wish I was a mole in the ground
Cause if I was a mole in the ground
I'd tear those mountains down
I wish I was a mole in the ground

Wish I was a lizard in the spring
Wish I was a lizard in the spring
Cause if I was a lizard in the spring
I'd make those mountains sing

Kempie let your hair hang down
Kempie let your hair hang down
Let your hair hang down let your bangs curl
    around
Kempie let your hair hang down

Kempie wants a nine dollar shawl
Kempie wants a nine dollar shawl

Well she come down the hill with a twenty
    dollar bill
Kempie where you been so long

I been in the pen so long
I been in the pen so long
Well I been in the pen with the rough and
    rowdy men
Kempie where you been

Wish I was a mole in the ground
Wish I was a mole in the ground
Cause if I was a mole in the ground
I'd tear those mountains down

Here it's a twenty-dollar bill—making the
image ordinary, making it present, making it not
strange. And Zagoren's singing—at a step back
from the song, drawing, her completely even
tone says, on lifetimes of reflection—does the
same, even more coolly. The slides in her voice,
from one word to another thinking everything
over with almost sing-songy lifts—"Cause if I
wuzz a lizz-ard ina spring"—draw on a completely modern, placeless, post-sixties accent,
from somewhere between the college and the
mall. The artlessness of it, the way she refuses or
doesn't bother to rise to certain notes, makes her

anyone, or you or me. And in this artless mall-rat manner, the song still claims the whole world. The tones from Zagoren's banjo rise and fall. Notes flip away from the melody. Nearly atonal echoes take you into a world that will never change, where the only possible engine of change is consciousness, the faculty that allows the creature who is singing to dream of what it cannot have. That is all on the surface, but the performance works on a subconscious level too. Shading the transitional phrases from the banjo are patting sounds, like footsteps, rooting the music in the ordinary and the everyday, and at the same time there is the most softly doomstruck bass sound imaginable, something between a barely fingered thump and a hum, adding to the sense of suspension in the music, of no time adhering to the performance at all. Even farther behind the singer you can hear cicadas. Finally the performance sounds like someone breathing in her sleep.

This really is a dream—a recording of a dream. And like Neuwirth, Zagoren adds her own wormhole. In Lunsford's version of the song, and in every other, Tempe—or Kempie—always wants a nine-dollar shawl, and the man singing comes over the hill waving his money, ready to get it for her. In Zagoren's song, it's Tempe herself—here as Kempie, a name, or a mishearing, that seems to have migrated into the song sometime in the 1960s—who comes over the hill, holding up a twenty-dollar bill. "Kempie," Zagoren follows, singing in the voice of the other person in the song, "where you been so long?"—and in American music, from Lead Belly's "Black Girl" to Buddy Holly's "Midnight Shift" and in countless songs before and after, "Where you been so long?" means only one thing: *Who have you been sleeping with?* The implication is that Tempe has been on the street to get the money for her shawl herself—which doesn't necessarily imply that that is anything Zagoren meant to say. There are unmarked doors in songs like "I Wish I Was a Mole in the Ground." That's how other songs dart in and out of it like thieves. The words can shift on your tongue without you knowing it. Notes can slip your fingers. Breaking and entering, the song can retrieve its words from your subconscious; notes can compose a melody you sense but don't hear. The song writes itself; Zagoren may have stumbled into something the song always wanted to say.

Still, if you knew Lunsford's version—which, with the *Anthology of American Folk Music* circulating through bohemian enclaves and folk-music scenes for more than fifty years before Zagoren took up the song, so many did—then her changing the forty-dollar bill to a twenty-dollar bill might not erase but highlight the oddness of the first reference. After all, who's ever heard of a forty-dollar bill?

After listening to the song for more than thirty years, it began to bother me. *What was the forty-dollar bill?* And, after thirty years, with the Internet, it was easy to find that as colonial currency, in Georgia, let alone as national currency, as issued by the Continental Congress, the forty-dollar bill was in circulation only a few years, from 1776 to 1779 or a year later. There were different variations. Some carried different names for the country behind it: "The United States of North America."

From the vantage point of two hundred and thirty-seven years, it looks tiny: less than three by less than two inches. But the design is still startling. A crude Masonic eye, with lines emanating from it, a ring of stars, an altar with a fire rising from burnt offerings upon it—burnt offerings that, a student explained to me, signified the covenant between Abraham and his descendants and Jehovah, but which here signify

the covenant of legal tender, the covenant between citizens and their government—all of it means that, like "World Upside Down," the line "I come o'er the hill with a forty-dollar bill" dates back to the Revolution.

We can dig up that knowledge; the song doesn't dig it up. As a friend pointed out, there were no railroads when there was a forty-dollar bill, but the song doesn't care about time. It presents the forty-dollar bill as if it were the most obvious thing in the world—and as if it is a riddle, or a red herring, a joke the song gets and we don't. But why does the reference remain in the song at all? Why didn't it drop away generations ago, when the existence of a forty-dollar bill had been completely erased from national memory? Is it because there is some passed-down, fabling memory of how, once, there really was a forty-dollar bill? Or because there is no such real memory, because the existence of the forty-dollar bill has been so completely forgotten that only the phrase remains, the phrase itself now riding the rails of a single song, as a floating signifier of its own strangeness? Because the reference has survived precisely because it communicates absurdity, unlikeliness, a world upside down, a world where a mole could root down a mountain? We're again in the realm of abstraction, where the song speaks both in plain language and in unknown tongues—and where any insistence that the song has a *real* meaning, a knowable meaning, would be the weirdest thing of all.

A few years ago, in a seminar in Minnesota, people were talking about "I Wish I Was a Mole in the Ground" when one person stopped the discussion cold. "I want to know what everybody thinks this song is about," he said. "*I* know," he said—"but I want to know what other people have to say before I tell you." Nobody said anything. The notion that this song could have a single meaning, a meaning that would shut the song up, that would stop it from making meaning, made no sense.

The student answered his own question. This is a southerner, he said, just after the Civil War, looking out at a world that has been turned upside down. The Federal government is the mountain, rising over him, blotting out the sun. The southerner is the mole. And if it takes all of his life and the lives of his descendants down ten generations, he will root that mountain down.

Think about it that way, and the song is anything but old, anything but history, except for the history that is at our fingertips. The song is a manifesto, speaking for Americans in the twenty-first century raising their voices to denounce the Federal government as a monster crushing the nation, and for countless others, American and not. *Like a mole in the ground,* said Edward Snowden, said Dzhokhar and Tamerlan Tsarnaev,★ said Chelsea Manning, said Daniel

★ "I been in the bin so long," wrote a friend in Watertown, Massachusetts, after his part of the Boston area was locked down during the house-to-house search for Dzhokhar Tsarnaev after the Boston Marathon bombings in 2013.

Ellsberg, said Kim Philby, said Leon Czolgosz, said Nathan Bedford Forrest, said John Wilkes Booth, said Harriet Tubman, said Thomas Paine, *I will root that mountain down.*

It doesn't matter that Bascom Lamar Lunsford was raised in a pro-Union part of North Carolina—in Marshall County, where in 1860 there were less than six thousand people, barely two hundred of them slaves, almost twenty black and free—any more than it matters that his father was a Confederate soldier, any more that in the face of a song as elusive as "I Wish I Was a Mole in the Ground," it matters that my father's mother, my grandmother, came from Alabama, and her father, my great-grandfather, buried just across the lane from Hank Williams in Oakwood Cemetery in Montgomery, was a Confederate captain, any more than it matters if one came to the United States after the Second World War. The song tells its own story, and then finds the singers to sing it.

In *Chronicles,* Bob Dylan talks about his education: about going to the New York Public Library and reading the newspapers from 1855 to 1865 on microfilm. "I wasn't so much interested in the issues," he says, "as intrigued by the language and rhetoric of the times." He talks about the country in utter disruption. "After a while," he writes,

you become aware of nothing but a culture of feeling, of black days, of schism, evil for evil, the common destiny of the human being getting thrown off course. It's all one long funeral song, but there's a certain imperfection in the themes, an ideology of high abstraction, a lot of epic, bearded characters, exalted men who are not necessarily good.

This, Dylan goes on to argue, is the what and the where and the when of the American folk song, of the American folk-lyric language: the language of, among other songs, "I Wish I Was a Mole in the Ground." Yes, there were earlier American folk songs that traveled with the frontier—"Springfield Mountain," "Omie Wise," the old English songs like "Lord Randall" still squirreled away in Appalachian hollows. But there was no critical mass. There was no point of explosion, where the rhetoric of the times shattered into fragments, and a new language took shape as a tool, a gift, a weapon that anyone could use, that anyone could take as his or her own. That, Dylan was saying, was because the national story that everyone knew, that everyone had once pretended to believe, had been torn up, then stitched back together out of joint, with new faces blinking in the light, and old faces, allegiances, identities, and beliefs no longer clear. Thus new stories are possible, and necessary. Old songs too break into fragments, and take on new words, new melodies, new rhythms. Dylan speaks of the "chilling precision" of folk songs, whole novels in a few lines, and, in that suggestive phrase, of a "certain imperfection in the themes," an opening, a place where a singer could drive through and map the country for him- or herself.

Suddenly, the form is available to all, attractive to all—and the whole notion of the all, of everything a song could say, of what it could hint at in coded phrases and evanescent melodies, had opened like a curtain rising over a national stage. With the freeing of the slaves, there is for a great part of the country a new freedom of movement, a whole sector of the population empowered to speak in public for the first time—to travel from town to town and sing on the streets. There is the opening of the West. The Civil War leads to huge concentrations of wealth and power, to the point where the Federal government becomes almost irrelevant, a mole underneath the mountains of trusts, monopolies, and railroad barons, an anti-democratic revolution side by side with a cryptically democratic revolution in speech, in song, in culture. In the 1890s, with the Klan ascendant in the old Confederacy, with *Plessy v. Ferguson* affirming racial segregation anywhere in the country, with African-Americans returned to a serfdom not that far from slavery, with the right of black Americans to vote gained after the Civil War suppressed across the South, the blues began to take shape. Labor songs and tramp songs emerged with the beginnings of organized labor, of strikes and strikes destroyed by mass murder and hired thugs. Symbolism begins to replace what can't be said out loud. The mole pokes its head out of the ground.

Not long ago, Bob Dylan talked about how lines in a song—including his own, lines like "The enemy I see wears a cloak of decency"— might be lies, or that might, as if of their own volition, lie, and lines in a song that can't lie. He argued that there was a crucial, fatal difference between a line that reaches a conclusion, or that even hints at anything specific, a moral, an ending, and a line that might not be obviously or intentionally vague, might not be absurd, but is somehow incomplete: a line that could be waiting for someone, like a new singer, to finish it, but more than that, a line resisting anyone's effort to finish it. A line that is, in the end, inviting you in, demanding that you assume one of the thousand faces in the song, or that you add your own face to it.

It might be that "I Wish I Was a Mole in the Ground" is more than a song that can't lie—because it's allegory, we might say, because it's so out of reach. It might be that the song is stranger than that. It may be a song that doesn't allow its singer to lie—but that too may be just a fantasy. In folk songs like "I Wish I Was a Mole in the Ground" or "The Coo Coo" or "Red Apple Juice" or "East Virginia" there is no original and no copy—but there was a man who learned to play the banjo and sing "I Wish I Was a Mole in the Ground" himself, who studied every printed version, a man who, his wife and his children sometimes complained, all but abandoned his profession and even his family in his pursuit of this song and others that spoke the same language. It's worth listening to him explain why, to sing "I Wish I Was a Mole in the Ground," you have to learn to let the song sing you. You have to learn to sing a song as strange as this one in the flattest, simplest voice.

What Bascom Lamar Lunsford said was almost exactly what Mark Twain once said about the American voice:

The humorous story is American, the comic story is English, the witty story is French. The humorous story depends for its effect upon the manner of the telling; the comic story and the witty story upon the matter.

The humorous story may be spun out to great length, and may wander around as much as it pleases, and arrive nowhere in particular; but the comic and witty stories must be brief and end with a point. The humorous story bubbles gently along, the others burst.

The humorous story is strictly a work of art—high and delicate art—and only an artist can tell it; but no art is necessary in telling the comic and the witty story; anybody can do it. The art of telling a humorous story—understand, I mean by word of mouth, not print—was created in America, and has remained at home.

The humorous story is told gravely; the teller does his best to conceal the fact that he even dimly suspects that there is anything funny about it; but the teller of the comic story tells you beforehand that it is one of the funniest things he has ever heard, then tells it with eager delight, and is the first person to laugh when he gets through. And sometimes, if he has had good success, he is so glad and happy that he will repeat the "nub" of it and glance around from face to face, collecting applause, and then repeat it again. It is a pathetic thing to see.

"Acting out the part [in a song] is offensive to one who knows," Bascom Lamar Lunsford said late in his life. "A fellow came by trying to learn a certain ballad. He put more into it than there was. He put unnecessary expressions to show his feelings of misfortune. Folks want to exaggerate what they know about something to impress you, when they know only certain outstanding features.

"Here's the idea. A song tells a story—tells something. The poetry is the message, and the music is the aid. A fellow ought to believe his own story, so to speak, no matter what it is. A man ought to sing it like it was a fact. Now for example:

John Henry was a little baby
Sittin' on his Papa's knee
He looked up to his Papa and he said,
The hammer'll be the death of me, Lord, Lord
The hammer'll be the death of me

"John Henry's a wonderful piece of music," Lunsford said. "It's a wonderful thing. So you sing it like you think it was a fact."

If there is an original of "I Wish I Was a Mole in the Ground," it's because once, in 1928, Lunsford was able to do that: to sing about moles and lizards, forty-dollar bills and nine-dollar shawls, railroads and curly hair, thugs and vampires, as if they were simple, obvious facts.

He knew the song was a mystery before and after it was anything else, and he knew it was mystery that he was passing on. As he did so, every time he sang the song—recording it not only in 1924 and 1928 but in 1935, 1936, 1946, 1947, 1948, 1949, 1951, and 1966, singing it for his mother just before she died and from the stage of his own folk festival long after that; for all the times he told the story of the night in 1936 when, thanks to the folk-music devotee Eleanor Roosevelt, he stood in the White House before the president of the United States and the king and queen of England to sing the songs of the Pigeon River Valley—Bascom Lamar Lunsford erased himself. He wished himself into the ground, and sent the song out into the world— where it is digging now, moving through time, in the dark, the mole as its own John Henry, the mountain the song's own steam drill. And finally, in one last reversal, if the mole is John Henry, then so, when he sang "I Wish I Was a Mole in the Ground," when he told a humorous story about how, as against an unlistening mountain, one person's voice might echo into infinity, was Bascom Lamar Lunsford his own John Henry. And that is one last face the song contains.

NOTES

Bob Dylan, "A folk song." *Chronicles, Volume One* (New York: Simon and Schuster, 2004), 71.

Bascom Lamar Lunsford, "I Wish I Was a Mole in the Ground" (Brunswick, 1928). Included on *Anthology of American Folk Music,* edited by Harry Smith (1952, as volumes 1–3, three sets of double LPs, in CD format Smithsonian Folkways, 1997, and remastered in LP format including Smith's originally unissued volume 4, Mississippi Records, 2014), and on Lunsford, *Ballads, Banjo Tunes, and Sacred Songs of Western North Carolina* (Smithsonian Folkways, 1996).

Robert Cantwell, "Smith's Memory Theater: *The Folkways Anthology of American Folk Music,*" *New England Review,* Spring/ Summer 1991. See also Cantwell, *When We Were Good: The Folk Revival* (Cambridge, MA: Harvard, 1996).

John Cohen, "A mystical god." Talk on Harry Smith, St. Mark's Church Poetry Project, November 10, 1995. Recording courtesy Rani Singh.

Walter Benjamin, "The Author as Producer" (1934), *New Left Review* 62, July-August 1970.

"I wish" variants ("I wish I was a bird in a tree," etc.) from a performance by Sara Beck, Danielle Durkin, Evan Glasson, Beth Schwartzapfel, and Todd Wright, 2007.

Lunsford "Mole" variants courtesy Jennie Rose Halperin, formerly of Columbia University's Center for Ethnomusicology.

Bob Dylan, "Memphis Blues Again," *Blonde on Blonde* (Columbia, 1966). See also Cat Power, "Stuck Inside of Mobile with the Memphis Blues Again," on *I'm Not There Original Soundtrack* (Columbia, 2007).

Bob Dylan, "All the Authorities." From interview with Nora Ephron and Susan Edmiston, "Positively Tie Dream," *New York Post,* September 26, 1965. Collected in *Bob Dylan: The*

Essential Interviews," edited by Jonathan Cott (New York: Wenner Books, 2006). Dylan's 1970 recording of "Little Brown Dog," as "Tattle O'Day," is included on *Another Self Portrait* (Columbia, 2013). "Nottamun Town" emerged in his music as the melody of "Masters of War" and as the lyric impetus behind "A Hard Rain's a-Gonna Fall"; see Greil Marcus, "Stories of a Bad Song," in *Bob Dylan by Greil Marcus: Writings 1968–2010* (New York: PublicAffairs, 2010).

Fred Moody, "I Wish I Was a Mole in the Ground," recorded by Frank C. Brown, 1921. Courtesy Todd Harvey, American Folklife Center, Library of Congress. Brown also recorded parts of twenty-two songs by Bascom Lamar Lunsford and many by other singers.

Bascom Lamar Lunsford, "I Wish I Was a Mole in the Ground" (Okeh, 1924). Courtesy Steve Weiss, Southern Folklife Collection, University of North Carolina.

Bascom Lamar Lunsford, "It was the last request." Introduction to "I Wish I Was a Mole in the Ground," Library of Congress archive, 1949. Courtesy Christopher King.

Bascom Lamar Lunsford, "I'm one of them." Commentary from Columbia University Library Recording, 1935. Courtesy Jennie Rose Halperin. Loyal Jones's *Minstrel of the Appalachians: The Story of Bascom Lamar Lunsford* (Boone, NC: Appalachian Consortium Press, 1984) includes a complete log of the hundreds of "Memory Collection" songs Lunsford recorded for Columbia in 1935 and the Library of Congress in 1949. For a sense of the breadth of Lunsford's musical world, see David Hoffman, *Music Makers of the Blue Ridge,* a 1964 National Public Television documentary where Lunsford, at eighty-two, acting the part of the country squire, takes a New York filmmaker on a tour of Madison County, introducing him to all the notable local musicians, ending with one Jesse Ray, or Lost John, who picks up his fiddle and plays a version of "Little Maggie" that can make your heart feel as if it's about to come out of your chest (reissued as *Bluegrass Roots,* Mira Entertainment). In 1989, for the PBS *American Experience* series, Hoffman made the less interesting biographical portrait *Ballad of a Mountain Man: Bascom Lamar Lunsford.*

Dylan, "It was all a mistake." *Chronicles,* 14.

Marianne Faithful, "Kimbie," *Easy Come, Easy Go—18 Songs for Music Lovers* (Naïve, 2009). Based on Jackson C. Frank's 1965 version of the song, where Tempe changes her name and the mole raises its head only in the last verse; see Jackson C. Frank, *Blues Run the Game* (Castle, 2003).

Bascom Lamar Lunsford, "The people of the countryside." In Lunsford, "Mine Own," *Southern Exposure,* January/February 1986. Courtesy Loyal Jones.

Bob Neuwirth and Eliza Carthy, "I Wish I Was a Mole in the Ground." Meltdown Festival, Royal Festival Hall, London, July 2, 1999, performance video included on *The Harry Smith Project: Anthology of American Folk Music Revisited* (Shout, 2006).

anbb (Alva Noto and Blixa Bargeld), "I Wish I Was a Mole in the Ground," *Mimikry* (Raster-Noton, 2010). "I wish I was a rat" is one exclamation that surfaces in the animal rampage of the second part of this performance. It's a displacing spectacle, with Bargeld singing "I been in the bend, so long," more than a century after Lunsford learned the song—what can people in 2010 think of these arcane references to nothing? But from another perspective, with Bargeld, a German with more than thirty years of avant-garde assaults and experiments behind him chanting the song to a severe, buzzing techno background as the Canadian sound artist Noto sits at keyboards to the side, the two together insist on a presentation of something absolutely modern. Bargeld is at first a machine, then psychotic, with always a trace of the stand-up comedian he once yearned to be. Other twenty-first-century treatments worth noting include Timber Timbre's "As Angels Do," from *Cedar*

Shakes (Timbertimbre.com, 2005) and Tallest Man on Earth, "I Won't Be Found," from *Shallow Grave* (Gravitational, 2008), both with swooningly alluring guitar picking. Which is not to ignore Zedenek Miller's Czech cartoon series *The Mole,* which in 1974 aired "The Mole and the Music," wherein the Mole, staring into the horn of a Victrola in his underground den, finds his favorite record broken. The only way to hear the song again is to put together a band and play it, which the mole and its fellow forest animals proceed to do. It's a straight rock treatment with a stentorian talked vocal: "I'm gonna take that mountain down / Cause it's there."

Cantwell, *When We Were Good,* 226.

Sindhu Zagoren, "Mole in the Ground," included on DJ Rupture, *Special Gunpowder* (Tigerbeat, 2004). Jace Clayton "added the bass/organ (it's computer generated), mixed a couple of vocal tracks and produced the song," Zagoren said in 2015. "I believe one of the overarching themes for his album, or at least that he was interested in at the time, was mixing acoustic instruments with computer-generated sounds." Cicadas recorded by Lawrence English.

Zagoren, "I experimented." To GM, 2011.

1778 Continental Congress forty-dollar bill from GM.

Matthew Schneider-Meyerson, "I want to know." University of Minnesota, 2008. In 2013, my friend Cyndy Karon, who grew up in Ohio with family ties to Appalachian Kentucky, heard the song slightly differently, but just as specifically: "This is so clearly a southerner who had to go north for factory work, yearning to return to the farms of his boyhood and his ancestors: *Even if I had to be a mole, it would be worth it to be back on the land.* And the mountain to be rooted down is the factory, the industrial north." But the image of the mountain is doubled, as nemesis and mirror: "The mountains are a hard environment that doesn't give anything easily, but it was also very much a part of who these people were, not just the source of their sustenance. It was a natural temple for them, and I think they cherished it that way."

Information on Marshall County from Bill Finger, "Bascom Lamar Lunsford: The Limits of a Folk Hero," *Southern Exposure,* Spring/Summer 1975, 29.

Bob Dylan, "I wasn't so much" and following: *Chronicles,* 84–85.

Bob Dylan, on songs and lies. See Luc Sante, "I Is Somebody Else," in *Kill All Your Darlings: Pieces 1990–2005* (Seattle: Yeti, 2007), 155. Sante draws on the interview with Dylan in Paul Zollo's *Songwriters on Songwriting,* expanded ed. (New York: Da Capo, 2003).

Mark Twain, "How to Tell a Story" (1897).

Bascom Lamar Lunsford, "Acting out the part." Quoted in Loyal Jones, *Minstrel of the Appalachians,* 136.

ACKNOWLEDGMENTS

Though this is a very short book, it's been taking shape for a long time, and there is some ground to cover.

My first thanks go to The William E. Massey Sr. Lectures in the History of American Civilization, under the auspices of which the chapters in this book were first given as talks at Harvard University in the fall of 2013. At Harvard I cherish the warm welcome and humbling introductions of John Stauffer, Werner Sollors, Carol Oja, and Ingrid Monson. I thank Kevin Higgins for impeccable and sometimes complex sound work, Arthur Patton-Hock for making everything easy, and Summer Shafer. I have worked with Lindsay Waters at Harvard University Press for more than thirty years, and it's been a pleasure to do so again, along with Amanda Peery and the designers Tim Jones and Peter Holm. My thanks go as well to Deborah Grahame-Smith, the production editor, Wendy Muto, and to Sue Warga for her careful and sensitive copy editing.

Putting aside Bob Dylan fandom in 1964, when I first heard "Ballad of Hollis Brown," and a obsessive fascination with Bascom Lamar Lunsford's "I Wish I Was a Mole in the Ground" dating to 1970 and with Geeshie Wiley's "Last Kind Words Blues" dating to 1994, the songs came together for me in an undergraduate lecture class called "Music as Democratic Speech— From the Commonplace Song to Bob Dylan," which I taught at the New School in New York in 2007 and from 2009 through 2014, and at the University of Minnesota in 2008. At the New School, I owe all sorts of debts to Robert Polito, and much to Lori Lynn Turner, Laura Cronk, Justin Sherwood, and Luis Jaramillo; at Minnesota I thank Paula Rabinowitz and Barbara Lenhoff. My New School TAs when I was first putting the class together—Beth Schwartzapfel, Todd Wright, Evan Glasson, Sara Beck, and Danielle Durkin—remain part of everything here, as do Jeff Johnson, Molly Gallentine, Jaclyn Lovell, and David McNamara from 2010. The students in the graduate seminars that spun off from the lectures are all over these pages, in countless ways, from anguished, raging, phantasmagoric papers to quizzical expressions and class performances: in 2012, Virginia Dellenbaugh, Maura Ewing, Chad Felix, Leigh Metzler, Joy Baglio, Matthew Choate, Jordan Depandahl, Michael DeSanti, Jean Garnett, Allison Kirkland, Kristin Steele, Liz Richard, Ida Tveldt, and Synne Borgen, and in 2014 Andreea Scarlat, Evan Thomas, Nicole Basta, Sarah Thomas, Sara Wilkins, Samuel O'Hana Grainger, Jordan Straubel, Corban Goble, Samir Benoaur, and Rania Dalloul. At the New School I took stories from Xan Price and a crucial interpretation from Gabriel Surin. I haven't forgotten Frankie Wagner's class performance of her spirit walk version of "I Wish I Was a Mole in the Ground."

The work here was played out at other forums as well, and at Berkeley I thank Kathleen Moran and Louise Mozingo of the American Studies Program, at Case Western Mary Davis and Duane Bible, and at Duke Megan Stein.

At Bob Dylan's office, Jeff Rosen was unfailingly helpful and generous, as was Callie Gladman. So were Eric Isaacson of Mississippi Records; Paula Ransom, representing the family of L.V. Thomas; and Jon Langford of the Mekons. I could never have followed the story of Geeshie Wiley without John Jeremiah Sullivan's truly heroic detective work, which broke decades of silence, and I will always remember his sharing his discoveries with me as they happened. Earlier on, and from then on, Robert Cantwell was there first. And for offering stories, facts, obscure publications, archived recordings, good talk, good advice, and much more, I thank Dean Blackwood of Revenant Records, Scott Blackwood, Daphne Brooks, Joe Bussard, Leslye Davis, Joel Finsel, Sophia Falcone, Emily Forland and Emma Patterson of Brandt and Hochman, Michael Goldberg, Jennie Rose Halperin, Howard Hampton, Todd Harvey of the American Folklife Center at the Library of Congress, Loyal Jones, Cyndy Karon, Christopher King, Doug Kroll, Jon Langford, Cecily Marcus at the Library of the University of Minnesota (and, as DJ Cecily on Radio K, for her discovery of the *Special Gunpowder* version of "Mole in the Ground"), Emily Marcus, Larry McMurtry, Bob Neuwirth, Steve Perry, Jeff Place of Smithsonian Folkways, Matthew Schneider-Meyerson, Marc Smirnoff, Dick Spottswood, Sarah Vowell, Robert Weil, Steve Weiss of the Southern Folklore Collection at the University of North Carolina at Chapel Hill, Jack White of Third Man Records, and Sindhu Zagoren.

And thanks to Jenny for the forty-dollar bill.

CREDITS

TEXT

Credits

Collected Poems of Richard Hugo by Richard Hugo. Used by permission of W. W. Norton & Company, Inc.

Jonathan D. Langford, "Geeshie." Reprinted with permission by Jonathan D. Langford.

Bob Dylan, "Memphis Blues Again." Copyright © 1966 by Dwarf Music; renewed 1994 by Dwarf Music. All rights reserved. International copyright secured. Reprinted by permission.

ILLUSTRATIONS

Marion Post Wolcott, August 1941. *Lame Deer (vicinity), Montana. Skull in front of Indian steam bath on Cheyenne Indian Tongue River Reservation to keep evil spirits away, a belief which is part of their "medicine."* Farm Security Administration/Library of Congress.

Photograph of woman standing on automobile. From the estate of L.V. Thomas. Used by kind permission of Paula Ransom. All rights reserved.

Marion Post Wolcott, November 1939. *Negroes Jitterbugging in a juke joint on Saturday afternoon. Clarksdale, Mississippi Delta.* Farm Security Administration/Library of Congress.

Continental Congress, 1778, 40 dollars. Collection of the author.

INDEX

Index

Index

Index

Index

Index

Index

Index